Ruby R

Once upon a time there w   _ girl called
Ruby Redd. When Ruby was born she was
quite ill and very small; she had to stay in
hospital until the doctors decided she was
strong enough to go home with her mother.
Ruby grew stronger as two years passed, but
she did not do the things that other children
did, that her brother, Ivan, did. She did not
smile at people, or hold out her arms to be
held. There were no games of "peek-a-boo" or
"wave-bye-bye"; no gazing into the eyes of
people and sharing fun. Ruby hated to be
held; she would hold herself stiffly, straining
away from whoever attempted to cuddle her
and closing her eyes.

As she grew older, instead of trying to copy
words Ruby shrieked and screamed, throwing
herself around the room in bursts of running
and jumping that continued until she collapsed
in exhaustion. Rather than playing with toys
Ruby would rock and try to bang her head. If
prevented from injuring herself in that way she
would attempt to bite her own hands or tear at
her hair. Only through constant distraction
with music and being offered small, usually
hard, items to hold would Ruby calm down at

all; filling her hands completely with such items and huddling over to study them in minute detail. She did not sleep but napped in fifteen-minute bursts watched by her parents turn-and-turn about as they slept in shifts.

Ruby was three before she spoke her first word clearly, 'Bocky',was as close as she could come to the sound of 'bottle'. Every new word took endless repetition to help her understand how to make the sounds herself; allowing her to put her fingers into an adult mouth to feel the shapes made by lips and tongue and then feel how to shape them in her own mouth seemed to help her. Her use of language was very limited and related only to immediate needs, she looked away and closed her eyes to avoid interaction with everyone and would often become distressed without there being any obvious cause.

Her parents sought advice from doctors and were told 'She's just slower to develop than her brother', 'You shouldn't push her, every child develops at their own pace' and 'these things take time'. The advice did not reassure them and did nothing to relieve Ruby's distress so they tried different things to see if they would help.

They changed the family's diet to remove any additives, they gave up work to concentrate on Ruby's needs and they tried as hard as they could to make their home a calm, happy place that would allow Ruby to relax.

By the age of four Ruby had very limited language, but was a little calmer, sleeping a little better and had begun to seek physical contact with others, even rarely choosing to meet their eyes or return a smile. She was able to attend a nursery but still refused to play with others Ruby was happy to be a 'living doll' for other little girls to play Mommy but showed no interest in trying to talk or play with them.

At her parents insistence Ruby was assessed and referred to a child development centre where she was diagnosed with special needs. From there her educational needs began to be discussed...

****

extract from a Medical report on a Child who may require Special Education:-

...Relevant factors in child's and family history:

Ruby was born via lower segmental Caesarean section due to maternal eclampsia. She was a small-for-dates baby and required special support in the Special Care Baby Unit. She reached most developmental milestones at the right time during her first year of life, but she gradually slipped behind, mainly in areas of language, speech and socialisation.

She has been regularly reviewed by the Child Development Centre staff. Dr Wyndham has regularly monitored her development and carried out investigations to find out the possible cause of this delay. The family history is unremarkable.

Description of child's medical condition with details of present treatment (if any). Relevant reports and/or results of special investigations (eg Audiogram) are attached to this form.

Ruby is a tall and pleasant 4-year-old girl who has serious disorders of communication. See attached Speech Therapist report.

She seems to immerse in a world of her own, paying little attention to people around her. She has great attraction for certain objects, particularly telephones. She could hold a pretend conversation through the phone using her own jargon. She has little speech comprehension and she failed on occasion to respond to her name, she has poor eye contact but no echolalia.

Ruby's fine manipulation is good, but she could only scribble with a pencil using her right hand. She has no limitations with gross motor skills. Ruby has frequent tantrums which have become gradually less frequent as she has grown older.

The physical examination of Ruby failed to show any significant abnormalities which could explain her apparent delay in communication, speech and social skills....

****

extract from a Speech and Language Therapy Advice for a Proposed Statement of Special Educational Need:-

...CURRENT COMMUNICATION ABILITIES

Attention and Play Skills

Ruby can attend well to activities that interest her. At home, she enjoys watching videos that she chooses. She likes to explore objects, e.g. taking them apart, finding out what kind of noise they make. She likes to look at objects that reflect light. She enjoys painting activities at nursery. Ruby is developing some early symbolic play, e.g. having a cup of tea, playing on a telephone. Her play is mainly self-related, although she may involve a member of the family.

Verbal Understanding

Ruby responds to instructions within the context of certain situations. Her ability to respond can be variable, according to her level of co-operation. She does react to other people's gestures and tone of voice, e.g. if being praised.

Ruby's use of eye contact is continuing to improve with members of her family. Her vocabulary is increasing, but she can be inconsistent in her use of words. She can use 2-3 word phrases, ie bad dog, I love you, shut up you.

Ruby tends to use jargon to herself and may sing tunes. She will pull people towards what she wants, occasionally she may point to something. She can respond to others, e.g. by saying 'bye' to them, and on other occasions she may not react to those around her. She can show frustration if she is not able to get her own way or make herself understood by frowning and hand clenching, to demonstrate anger, progressing to tantrums if still not understood.

FUTURE COMMUNICATION NEEDS

Ruby needs to be involved with children who have normal communication abilities. The staff must have good understanding of communication disorder and will require support from a Speech and Language Therapist....

****

Dear Mr & Mrs Redd,

ASSESSMENT OF SPECIAL EDUCATIONAL NEEDS

Following Ruby's recent interview with the Headteacher of Upham School, I am pleased to advise you that Ruby may commence at the school on 13th September of this year. You will be notified of transport arrangements as soon as possible, (probably late August).

The process of assessing Ruby's educational needs has now been carried out. On the basis of the information obtained, it is considered that Ruby has special educational needs which require the support of a statement.

The next step is to let you have the proposed statement and you will find this enclosed in duplicate. Attached to it you will find copies of all the advice which I have received and which has been taken into account when considering Ruby's needs.

If you agree with the proposed statement will you please sign one copy and return it in the envelope provided within 15 days of receipt of this letter. Please keep the other copy and all the attached papers for reference. When I have your agreement I will send you a final copy.

If you disagree with any part of the proposed statement please contact Mr Lessor in this office within 15 days. It would be preferable for this to be done in writing.

Within the same period you may also request a meeting with an officer of this department to discuss your concern in which case you may like to telephone (Innsmouth 385511) for an appointment.

If you do not respond within 15 days it will be assumed that you are in agreement with the proposed statement and a final copy will be sent.

Yours sincerely,
Mr B. Lessor
for Area Education Officer

****

extract from proposed statement of special educational needs:-

...*SPECIAL EDUCATIONAL NEEDS*

Ruby is a healthy, happy child and is able to play well on her own. Although she does not involve herself in social play at school she is reported to imitate other children's activities at home. She plays with her older brother at home but finds it difficult to relate to anybody other than family members.

Ruby is experiencing a severe communication disorder with associated developmental delay. Her speech is relatively limited, with up to 50 words, but she is now beginning to be able to put two words together. She is able to follow some simple instructions and when looking at books is able to identify some pictures of common objects and likes to associate noises with the pictures.

Ruby needs a small group environment where she can have an individual language development programme to stimulate and develop her communication skills.

Ruby needs help to develop verbal concepts. She needs help to begin to develop social skills and to continue to improve self help and personal care skills, leading to more independence in these areas. Ruby needs individualised help to prepare her for the early stages of the National Curriculum which will allow her practice and reinforcement at each learning step.

It will be important to help build and maintain Ruby's self-esteem and confidence in both learning and social situations.

SPECIAL EDUCATIONAL PROVISION

Ruby will attend a special school able to offer her individualised programmes in language development and high levels of adult support from teachers who are experienced in teaching children who experience all round cognitive delays.

Further advice will be taken from other professionals who are experienced in working with children who have speech and language difficulties...

****

Dear Mr and Mrs Redd,

I am delighted to be able to tell you that your daughter, Ruby, has been accepted for a place at Upham school Nursery starting in September of this year. I have received her details from Hill Street Nursery, her assessment from the Child Development centre and the educational psychologist's report.

As you are aware Upham school addresses special educational needs and our staff are trained to assist severely learning disabled pupils with complex physical and mental needs. These include pupils, like your daughter, whose needs form part of the autistic spectrum and we offer placements from 4-16 years. If you have any questions or concerns please do not hesitate to contact me.

We look forward to seeing Ruby on 13th

September.

Yours sincerely,
        Melvin Moylan
        Headmaster

            ****

Monday, 13th September

Hi, Mr & Mrs Redd, I'm Honor, nursery manager. We met at the new entrants meeting in July. I thought I'd write and let you know how things have gone for Ruby on her first day, we'll send you little notes each day in this book and would appreciate if you could share any information or messages with us the same way.

Ruby's first day in Upham school nursery has been fine; she's enjoyed exploring the room and has played with lots of different toys. She even sat on Leila's (one of my assistants) lap of her own choice and pulled an arm around her shoulders for a cuddle.

Lunchtime was mainly spaghetti and after lunch Ruby played with the toy farm and had lots of tries with games on the computer. I know you warned us about her being reluctant to put down her 'treasures' and her hands have stayed full of her little toys all day which does restrict what she can do, but she seems happier with her hands full of familiar objects.

We had several attempts to persuade her to use the potty when we changed her nappy but she seemed reluctant to accept this and we've left this alone to give her a chance to settle in. Hope all goes well tonight.

Hi Honor, glad to hear all went well and Ruby came home tired and had a very good night's sleep. We can rarely persuade her to release her toys and have her hands free to use even asleep she tends to clutch things like her toy mermaid and a car or two. It would be nice if between us we could get her to at least hold onto fewer items as they limit what she is able to do with her hands.

Tuesday, 14th September

Aggie (I'm afraid I loathe my proper name;

Agatha, ugh! I much prefer my nickname) -
Ruby woke in a lovely mood today and made
several spontaneous comments about our cat,
Fleur, and her breakfast. Only single words
but it was exciting that she seemed to be
making an effort to communicate.

**Honor here, thank you for your comments
they were helpful in letting us know how
Ruby was likely to be during the day,
particularly that she was not tired or
grumpy! She's been fine today played
with quite a wide variety of toys and took
part in some 'classwork' on a one-to-one
basis with Leila, which gave us a chance
to start trying to find out what she can
do. One project was a lovely collage
picture and she seemed to love tearing
apart magazines and sticking pictures
together in ways that pleased her.**

**Ruby ate crisps at snack-time and took
part in movement exercises in the main
hall where she seemed to really enjoy
travelling around in all the free space.
She may be tired after all this activity!**

We suspect Ruby was a little over-tired to be
honest she chose to go to bed early but we

were up and down with her all night. I'm not surprised she enjoyed tearing up magazines as I spend a lot of time at home persuading her to NOT do that as she likes to rip off pieces and eat them. Glad to hear she wasn't doing that for you!

Wednesday, 15th September

Aggie - A brighter mood today: Ruby was playful whilst getting washed and dressed (Mom got soaked!) and she was enjoying creating a mess so much we had to coax her to calm down and eat before the bus came for her.

Sorry to hear about your soaking! Ruby had calmed down by the time she reached Nursery and took part in some craft-work with Leila. She seemed to really enjoy shaping and glueing soft grey material to make a mouse different textures appeal to her a lot, don't they? She enjoyed mimicking an eek eek sound for the 'mouse'.

A success at lunchtime as she consented to putting down her 'treasures' at lunch time so that she could feed herself.

Ruby made a good meal of fish fingers, potatoes and peas and showed some attention for what other staff and children were doing. She has sometimes been looking at people very intently as if trying to learn our faces but is still looking away if you catch her eye.

Swimming tomorrow

We're very pleased to hear about your success with persuading her to put down her toys but I'm afraid Ruby was rather unsettled when she came home. Watched videos and played games until 2a.m. when she finally fell asleep. However, it was good quality sleep once she was down and with fewer disturbances than she usually has.

Thursday, 16th September

Aggie - Ruby a bit grumpy this morning but did cheer up when her favourite cereal appeared for breakfast. She was looking for the bus with me today, waiting to be picked up for nursery.

Leila here, how do you both stay awake until 2a.m.? Ruby LOVED swimming; completely at home in the water and

wore armbands for support without any problem at all (I know you were both concerned she wouldn't like them but she was fine).

She put down her toys at lunchtime but did get slightly cross with me for asking her to do so. Afterwards we did some work together I've been organising this in short bursts as that seems to help Ruby stay focused and to help her to be less distractable. We also did a lot of small singing sessions and I was so surprised to hear what a lovely little voice she has! She seems to catch the 'rhythm' of the words even if not able to pronounce them quite correctly.

Much, much calmer night tonight; maybe singing helped? She was quite mellow and asked for bed at 10pm, settled relatively quickly and only had a couple of night-time wakes.

Friday, 17th September

Aggie - A good night's sleep obviously suited her because Ruby ate well and was in a really good mood. Woke up smiling, kept grinning

and wanted games as soon as she
got out of bed.

(As to how we stay awake that comes with lots
and LOTS of practice. There was a time we
regularly slept in 'shifts' to keep up and we still
resort to that when she goes through one of
her 'disturbed' phases).

**Leila here, everything fine today: the
good mood seems to have lasted. She
was so relaxed I managed to coax her to
put down her little toys between 12 and 2
so that she could eat lunch and then
carry out some activities afterwards.
Ruby appeared to accept this quite well.**

Horrible, horrible weekend I'm afraid. Ruby
kept demanding to go to nursery and refused
to accept any substitute we offered and so
we've had lots of tantrums. But, we know she
often goes through really difficult behaviour
just before she makes progress of some sort;
as if she can only move forward by regressing
in her behaviour. We're used to holding on in
the hope that some new behaviour or ability
will appear.

Her sleep pattern has disappeared so we're

sleeping in shifts again, at least it means neither of us has to get into a cold bed but early hours of the morning can seem to drag on forever when she's still running around!

Monday, 20th September

Aggie - Ruby still very disturbed this morning and her appetite is all over the place she begged for a bag of crisps and we compromised on a few crisps with an apple and milk. Maybe not the healthiest of breakfasts but at least there's some nutritional value in there. She was very anxious to get to school today repeated the word three separate times and kept going to the window to see if the bus was here yet.

Hi, Renee here Ruby asked for crisps at drinks time too! They're obviously a favourite of hers. We've had a very good day together; she's joined in on all the activities although her hands being full (I'm afraid she's clutching onto them despite coaxing) made it a bit difficult to manage some things! We had a lovely time at swimming, she's very confident in the water and (thankfully) she was prepared to put down toys to have her

hands free to paddle. Although everything was picked up again as soon as she left the water. Honor is out on a training day today but will be back tomorrow if you want to speak to her at all.

Whatever activities you did today obviously tired her out Ruby came home much calmer and happier and with a good appetite for her tea (and no demands for crisps!). We had a quieter evening and she asked for bed about 10.30 and went to sleep quite quickly and slept through. Bliss!

Tuesday, 21st September

Aggie - Another day of not seeming to want her breakfast but Ruby did manage an apple and a large glass of milk. She was in a very playful mood and spontaneously came and sat on both mine and Adam's (Daddy's) laps at different times. Lots of chatter but very hard to make out any real words.

Honor here, Ruby has had a good day in nursery; she has sat very nicely when asked and taken part in all the activities although her concentration can waver

at times. She did some excellent individual work with Thelma; very much enjoyed mixing paints and seemed to know what she was doing, fascinated by the colours and the effects of mixing them.

Ruby had a good lunch and afterwards went to the sensory room where she enjoyed watching and exploring all of the lights and shapes. We had a PE session in the main hall and Thelma persuaded her to put down most of her toys although one of the soldiers remained in her very firm grip throughout.

A nice evening Ruby quite tired but seemed to enjoy teasing Dad. She kept stripping off all her clothes despite our best efforts and saying, "Ruby cold, Ruby cold" and pointing at the fire. Since she'd made such an effort to use language to indicate what she wanted we put the fire on and coaxed her into pyjamas. She asked for bed shortly after 11 and slept relatively well with just a couple of disturbances.

Wednesday, 22nd September

Leila here, Ruby has had a wonderful day

today. We've been printing autumn leaves, cutting them out and glueing them into a big collage for the main hall. Ruby did language and singing work today which she seemed to enjoy a great deal; we had some beautiful smiles and she even gave me a cuddle!

Glad she's had such a good day. Sorry not to comment for the morning but we were late out of bed today and everything was a bit chaotic! More relaxed tonight, in a happy, playful mood and went to bed about 10.

Thursday, 23rd September

Aggie - Sorry, a truly horrible night. The man who lives over the road has a motorbike he parks outside and about 2am we were all woken by a recorded alarm saying, "This bike is being stolen. This bike is being stolen. Call the police." On and on and on.

After about 10 minutes it cut out and we soothed Ruby back to sleep. About half an hour later the alarm goes off again, and then again and again. Four times in all and Ruby was shrieking the place down by then.

While I was trying to calm her Adam opened our bedroom window and shouted down, "Whoever's nicking the bike I'll even give you a hand pushing it down the road if you'll take the b***** thing away and let us all get some sleep!"

Whereupon the idiot over the road starts yelling at Adam that he'll report him to the police. Adam told him straight that if he didn't turn that damned alarm off and stop disturbing Ruby he'd be calling the police for a lot more than a shouted comment!

Finally everybody calmed down and the alarm was turned off so we could settle Ruby again and we got her back to sleep at about 3.45am.

Unfortunately this late night (or early morning?) meant we overslept until about 8 and Ruby is still very tired. She had little appetite and her stomach seems to be slightly upset. The bike (unfortunately) is still parked across the road.

Honor here, sorry to hear about your dreadful night. Ruby does seem tired and not really 'with it' today. She's quite vague and dreamy but did take part in

some activities. Her stomach has settled and she had a good lunch so let's hope a good night's sleep settles her down again.

Ruby SO tired. She was nodding off during her meal and fell asleep as I washed and changed her. Tucked up in bed for 9 and only disturbed a couple of times when I had to change her.

Friday, 24th September

Aggie - The sleep obviously helped (especially since no alarms went off!) and Ruby was so cosy she was reluctant to get up today. Bright enough once I did get her moving and she's eaten a good breakfast and has been looking out for the bus.

Mandy here, Ruby attended assembly today and sat very well. She seemed to enjoy joining in the singing most of all.

Later, in PE, Ruby was furious with me because I insisted she put down her 'treasures' to take part in the exercises. She screamed, shouted and slapped at me but I just told her, put them down or you can't join in, and refused to give in.

Eventually she put them down and, grumbling, joined in with everybody else. I don't think she likes me very much after that!

It's been a very good week for Ruby and we've seen lots of work and interacting with staff and other children she's usually a sunny soul and I don't think we can hold one tantrum against her.

Hope you have a good weekend.

I'm afraid your good wishes were wasted although we do appreciate the thought. Ruby has given us a horrible time; we've taken her out for more walks, my sister,Becca, drove us to Pepperam House for a huge walk but Ruby has still constantly nagged for nursery.

Attending nursery has become her latest little obsession and no substitute will be accepted! That's Ruby all over; once she latches onto something she fixates on it to the exclusion of all else and you just have to hang on and ride it out. We've seen this behaviour so many times and it's early days yet so we hope she will settle down and probably start fixating on something else!

Monday, 27th September

Aggie - My, my what a difference. As soon as 'school' clothes appear Ruby became a different girl; big grins and cuddles all around. She ate a very good breakfast and drank milk, not keen on an apple so I substituted an orange which seemed to appeal rather more. She became a little anxious as the bus was slightly late but no major issues. Hope all goes well today.

Leila here, very sorry to hear about your weekend I wonder what it is she particularly likes about nursery, although it's very gratifying to know she does! She was very good at lunchtime; seemed particularly taken with the tomatoes and took Debbie's hand to get herself some more when she had finished.

It was hard work when I wanted her to practice some hand control work. Do you have any particular technique for persuading her to put her toys down when you want her to do something different?

Could we have a new toothbrush please?

Ruby obviously enjoyed herself today because she came home so mellow; we had a lovely, relaxing evening and although late to bed she slept very well.

Tuesday, 28th September

Aggie - The nice mood continues! Ruby cooperated with washing and dressing today (sometimes it's like trying to dress an eel!) and ate a very good breakfast with minimal spills and throwing. She's generally smiling, happy and playful so I hope that stays true for the rest of the day.

I will sort out a new toothbrush for tomorrow; I usually keep spares but I've run through them all.

Ruby tends to be very hard to them because although she'll have a good attempt at cleaning her teeth she grinds down on the brush if you're not careful. If she refuses to let go the brush I usually hold her nose until she lets go. PLEASE DON'T put your fingers in her mouth for any reason other than choking or emergency; in the wrong mood she will clamp down and grind her teeth and she's drawn blood with me many times. I'd hate for her to injure anybody.

Getting small toys or other items off Ruby is a problem, I know. Usually we get down on a face-to-face level, touch the object we want her to release and then hold out our hands and say, "Please, Ruby. Thank you."   She identifies this phrase with an exchange of objects or change of activities and usually complies. Honestly, sometimes this does not work and we resort to outright bribery, "Ruby have the apple. Mommy have the toys." If all else fails simply take away the objects and put them out of sight. Ruby will be annoyed and upset but she can be calmed down (eventually) with a lot of cuddles and being told, "Toy gone. Ruby play with this/do this instead."

Sorry about the length of this but it seems unfair not to tell you everything we can that can help keep her settled and happy.

Calming tantrums is an art-form in itself and you have to learn to judge what will work best in any given situation. Tickles and cuddles will often make her giggle and lose track of what she's annoyed about, but not always. You can pretend to cry which will usually make her run over to kiss and cuddle you 'better'. (I know it's a rotten trick but on bad days it can help where all else has failed).

Hi, Honor here. Thanks for all your information, don't worry about sending us long messages it helps us immeasurably to know more about Ruby and how you meet her daily needs.

Ruby has put down her toys twice today once <u>very </u>well and once quite well, which allowed her to take part in more things. She's been very cooperative and appears to be happy today. I'm on a course for the next 2 days and Leila will be taking over for me.

Ruby's good mood continued and she had a nice night. Settled to sleep late but rested well.

Wednesday, 29th September

Aggie - That good mood is still lasting. Ate cereal and yoghurt and asked for milk which she drank with a lot of smiles. Quite cuddly today and sat on my lap to look at pictures.

Hi, Leila here. Afraid we're a little pushed with Honor away and an assistant ill but Ruby has had a good day. She's clung to her toys but has joined in with singing and games despite this. In general a very happy and busy day. Hydro tomorrow and I hope you have a good evening.

Early evening went well but later on we had some noisy drunks sitting on our step (an all-too-frequent problem if you live above an off-licence) which Adam had to chase off when they started fighting and disturbing Ruby. Despite this she finally got off to sleep 11ish and only woke for a couple of changes.

Thursday, 30th September

Aggie - Apparently a good sleep gave her an appetite and Ruby ate very well. In a smiley mood today; big beaming grins about nothing in particular. Hope she has a good day and enjoys hydro.

Hi, Leila here. Ruby took part in all the activities today and had a nice session in hydro once we persuaded her to part with her toys. She's done some very good

sticking pictures today which we'll send home with her later.

Ruby was a little tired tonight she became rather dreamy and vague after tea and asked for bed about 9.30. Several changes overnight but settled back to sleep fairly easily afterwards.

Friday, 1st October

Aggie - Smiles and cuddles again today. Ruby wolfed down breakfast and demanded an extra banana, then stationed herself by the window to keep an eye out for the bus!

Hi, Honor here. We're short on staff today so just a quick comment to say Ruby has had a very good day, lots of activities and more eye contact than usual.

Hope you have a good weekend.

Quite a good weekend despite Ruby having a little sniffle. She finally appears to have accepted that days off for the weekend don't mean that nursery has gone awayand so she is not looking for the bus and asking, "Nurs'y?

Nurs'y," all the time. Apparently making sure she gets trips out for walks and to the park are quite acceptable, thank you.

On Sunday Adam and I took her with Ivan (her brother) to visit a car boot (Adam's a bit of a fan). Ruby stopped at one stall selling toys and after great consideration she picked up a doll set and said, "This. Please." It's the first time she has ever made a decision like that and she asked so nicely!

Monday, 4th October

Aggie - Ruby still a little sniffly but no temperature or upset stomach so we're sending her in as she's so looking forward to "Nurs'y." I've given her a dose of medicine to try to help with her nose which is a little drippy. If there are any problems please call and let me know.

Thelma here, Ruby has been fine today, doesn't seem bothered by her cold although we have had a couple of sneezes. Lots of work and interaction but her appetite was off; she rejected her main course and just ate fruit, but lots of it.

We gave Ruby the chance to swim and she wanted to take part but only managed half an hour. I made sure her hair was thoroughly dry afterwards and she seems fine if a bit snuffly. Hope she's feeling better tomorrow.

Ruby made up for her lack of appetite at lunch; I'd cooked chicken for tea and she wolfed it down as if she hadn't eaten in a week.

I suspect that cold is now history. An early night (9ish) but several changes as a slight cough caused a little stress incontinence.

Tuesday, 5th October

Aggie - No longer snuffling but Ruby was in a very tense and irritable mood at first. Picky about eating breakfast and remained difficult until nursery clothes were produced when she became all smiles and cuddles.

Honor here, today has been very good. Ruby seems to have thrown off her cold already and has been surprisingly amenable. She hasn't played with her little toys as much but rather paid

attention to what is going on in the nursery.

She handed over her toys on request to eat lunch and spent the whole afternoon without them - took part in many more activities with her free hands!

Tomorrow is our Harvest festival and we look forward to seeing you and all the other parents for our assembly.

What a nice evening! Ruby made a good meal, enjoyed some games and TV and was in bed asleep for 9.30. She must be saving her energy for tomorrow.

Wednesday, 6th October

Aggie - We're feeling very positive about today. Ruby cooperated by putting down her toys on request so that she could wash and dress, ate a good breakfast and left the toys lying on a chair whilst she shared cuddles with us both. That truly doesn't happen a lot and it was a lovely change. Look forward to seeing you and other staff tomorrow.

Honor here, nice to see you today.

Ruby a little over-excited before assembly but calmed down nicely as you saw. She did enjoy the singing, didn't she? Such a pretty voice!

After the parents left Ruby got on as normal so I don't think having her routine changed was too difficult for her. She was a little cross after lunch but none of us were quite sure what that was about.

Ruby was very helpful afterwards; came with me to collect a television and helped push it up the corridor then thoroughly enjoyed the video we all watched together.

An exciting evening for Ruby as my sister, Becca, took us all out to watch a magic show. I'm not sure how much Ruby understood but she loved the lights and music and a trip in auntie's car never fails to please. She went straight to sleep once we got home and slept almost straight through.

Sadly I must admit her voice is nothing to do with Adam or I, we both scare the crows when we try to sing. My mother, however, has a gorgeous singing voice so I assume it skipped a generation.

Thursday, 7th October

Aggie - Ruby up bright and early in a lovely, calm mood. She ate a very good breakfast and then sat by the window waiting for her bus.

Leila here, Ruby still in a nice mood in the nursery, not so many activities but lots of concentration.

Didn't eat much lunch but enjoyed her swimming trip. Is there any reason she's so lacking interest in food?

No, no reason we could think of for her lack of appetite but she refused most of her tea as well. However, I cooked sausage-in-a-blanket for supper and these were gobbled up as I don't make them very often! Asleep before 11 and only roused for a couple of changes overnight.

Friday, 8th October

Aggie - We had some major histrionics today; I foolishly tried to give Ruby the same breakfast cereal as her dad and brother which was wrong, wrong, wrong. Calmed her down and offered her regular cereal and she suddenly became cheerful and cooperative again. Not, however, before telling me I was a, "Bad, Mommy. BAD!" I consider myself well and truly told off and won't do that again.

Leila here, Ruby does like her own way, doesn't she? We've had some lovely interaction today; messing with paints obviously suited her mood because she refused some of the other activities she usually enjoys to keep painting.

Very successful lunch; not only handed over her toys without being prompted but also ate her meat something she tends to treat with great suspicion when she eats with us.

Ruby had us all laughing today as she became annoyed with a toy she was playing with and gave it a stern-but-calm talking to. Although few of the words were understandable we all recognised Honor-dealing-with-naughty-behaviour and had to smile. She's an amazing mimic.

I know what you mean about mimicry she

gives me a glare sometimes that is the spitting image of her auntie Becca's.

A pretty good weekend despite Ruby deciding to be naughty on more than a few occasions. She has her father's sense of humour and likes to tease but doesn't know when to stop!

Monday, 11th October

Aggie - Rather a quiet morning today; Ruby is playful but a little dreamy. It's almost as if she's still not quite awake.

Honor here, Ruby has become more lively as the day has gone on but has been very cooperative she actually chose to put down her little toys today and didn't pick them up until almost home time. She sat very nicely for group work and had some nice interactions with staff and other children.

In the afternoon she thoroughly enjoyed swimming; she was laughing and splashing about with great delight. We're keeping a close eye on her at the moment because she appears to be fascinated by anything electrical and

worries us a little with her interest in sockets.

I know what you mean about sockets. I've bought packets of those socket protectors because she seems interested in trying to poke things inside. If you need any just let me know; so far she's failed to work out how to remove them.

A good night to begin with Ruby happily ate her meal, played some games, watched videos and went down for about 10.30. Unfortunately about 1.30am the alarm was triggered and we could hear intruders in the off-licence below. After the recent news stories about properties being set on fire to destroy evidence from break-ins Adam became worried they might set light to the shop. With all the alcohol it would be like sitting on top of a bomb for us and so he threw on some clothes and rushed downstairs to try to chase them off.

He was down in time to see two of them run away but a third pulled out something which glinted (and he thought might be a knife) and took a swing at him so Adam hit him with the poker I'd handed to him for protection. The third man ran off as a police car arrived.

I know I mentioned in passing when we first met you that we get a lot of triggered alarms, usually drunken idiots who dash off as soon as the noise starts but this was rather nastier.

We have them so frequently I've got in the habit of making drinks for the policemen as they're taking statements/checking locks. Luckily it was two of our regulars guys because Adam (without thinking) told them about hitting the wannabe-burglar with the poker and PC Two-sugars-and-a-dash-of-milk-thanks quickly said,

"Oh, I'm sorry, Mr Redd, my ears are playing up tonight. Did you say you shouted loudly and the man ran away?"

Hastily Adam agreed and that's what was written down. Just as well or I suppose we'd see Adam in trouble for trying to defend himself from an armed robber! Crazy world!

Anyway, as you can imagine Ruby was very disturbed by all this and didn't go back to sleep until almost 4am.

Tuesday, 12th October

Aggie - After her disturbed sleep Ruby is very tired and is very dreamy. She honestly looks as if she could nod off but insists she wants to go to nurs'y If she does need to come home then call us and we'll come and pick her up.

Leila here, Ruby has stayed a little quiet but quite happy to take part in activities. She made a reasonable lunch and brightened up during the afternoon. I do hope you have a better night with Ruby and no further alarms.

We're all glad to hear that Adam was safe after such a terrifying encounter you read about things like that in the papers but never expect to encounter it in people you know.

Ruby nodding off over her tea tonight and so we've given her an early night. Settled and asleep before 8. Fortunately no further alarms overnight!

Wednesday, 13th October

Aggie - A good quality sleep has done her the world of good and Ruby is in a lovely, mellow mood. She managed cereal, fruit and milk for breakfast and was amazingly patient when the bus was a little late.

Honor here, Ruby in SUCH a good mood today. She was delighted with the Mickey Mouse game we introduced her to on the computer she started singing along with the songs and giggling.

We had a little trouble persuading her to give somebody else their turn on the computer but when Leila offered to draw things for her Ruby agreed. She asked for lots of items apple, shoes, cat, baby cat and dog and some of the requests got rather complicated for Ruby to be able to ask for clearly, she was putting together words to try to describe what she wanted eg baby + cat instead of kitten. Leila could barely draw fast enough to keep up.

Not much appetite today and reluctant to release her toys. Perhaps that break-in disturbed her more than we realised.

I think you may be right about Ruby; she was not only difficult to get to sleep but also seemed to be waking up with nightmares. It's awful when this happens because she seems to really struggle to realise she's awake and the nightmare is over; she was so shaken at one point we got her up and kept her awake to let her recover.

Thursday, 14th October

Aggie - Very, very tired today. I've tried to persuade her to stay at home but Ruby insists on "Nurs'y" so no dice there. Please don't hesitate to call us if she needs to sleep again, we'll bring her home by taxi if necessary.

Thelma here, Ruby quite dreamy but very happy to be here. We've given her a relaxed day; just one or two of her favourite activities. Little interest in food and lots of yawning toward the end of the day.

What a tired girl! She had a nap before tea, ate a little and played for an hour then insisted on bed. Luckily Ruby seemed to only have good dreams as no more waking up crying and shaking. She barely woke up either time I had to change her.

Friday, 15th October

Aggie - Ruby awake in good time and very hungry. Ate a very good breakfast but became grumpy when I was trying to get her washed and dressed. However, when I explained that if she did not hurry she would miss the bus she said, "Come on. Come on!" She ended up dressed and ready in record time and waited quite patiently for the bus.

Honor here, Ruby has been fine today. She seems far less interested in her selection of little toys and objects, we've noticed. Perhaps it helped her to cope with things initially until she could settle?

Ruby did some puzzles first thing and then we all went to a fantastic assembly which was all about music which we all loved. Her next activity was PE followed by language work. She made a good lunch and then had outside play since we had such nice weather to enjoy. Ruby was particularly pleased with our music activities where she had a turn with the tap-it box which she really likes. In the late afternoon we had a walk to church

and visited the pet shop where Ruby was very taken with 'baby cats'. I do hope you all have a good weekend.

Aggie - The weekend went well until Sunday. Ruby had Adam and I awake with her in shifts throughout the night and only fell asleep around 5.30am.

Monday, 18th October

Aggie - Well, despite her very late night Ruby work up as normal for 8am and went straight into her normal routine. She has eaten well and seems lively enough but after so little sleep I can't imagine she'll not feel tired and I'm sure she'll be flagging by the afternoon.

Honor here, sorry to hear about Ruby's bad night but she shows no particular sign of being tired. She's done some work on puzzle solving and hand control and had some nice 1-to-1 interaction. At lunch she absolutely adored tinned tomatoes and kept asking for more.

Ruby looking a little tired but not especially so. I know what you mean about tinned tomatoes; for last Halloween I made a dish called Dead

Man's brains which is basically mashed potato mixed with tinned tomatoes and Ruby couldn't get enough of it. Adam commented it was like watching a zombie movie because she kept demanding "Brains!" Quite a good night, Ruby asleep by 9 and only needed one change.

Tuesday, 19th October

Aggie - I'm afraid I'm back to being Bad Mommy; we've run out of pull-up pants and I've had to use one of Ruby's emergency nappies for her today and she's not very pleased with me about it. I have apologised because there's no excuse, I was over-tired and forgot but Ruby is NOT pleased. Otherwise; she's eaten a good breakfast and after an initial grumpy start has cheered up a great deal.

By the way, it's not just tinned tomatoes Ruby loves. She eats fresh ones like apples when she can but the mess is indescribable!

Leila here, Ruby happier once she had changed into pull-up pants and made some effort to use the toilet. She has been fine today. A nice individual

session with craft and play activities and work on the computer. Ruby really enjoyed finger-painting and made a hat. Today she cooperated for about half the PE session but then decided she'd had enough and went to look at pictures!

Ruby quite tired tonight (delayed reaction?) and was asleep before 10, barely rousing for her couple of changes overnight.

Wednesday, 20th October

Aggie - Ruby extremely hungry today she ate cereal and banana then demanded yoghurt and another banana afterwards with two drinks of milk. Not sure what that's all about but her initial grumpiness brightened up enough that she was demanding games and cuddles while we waited for the bus.

Thelma here, lots of good work from Ruby today. She did some sticking (we had quite a fight to stop her eating the glue!), a long session of outside play, craft-work, singing and language work. She's very happy and playful.

Ruby settled quite well (10.30) but was up

again between 12-3. This may be because we've had to change her bed and she really hates it when we make any changes in her routine or surroundings.

Thursday, 21st October

Aggie - Rather a grumpy start today (not surprising; we're both grouchy on so little sleep) but Ruby did cheer up once she had eaten.

Honor here, Ruby was her usual happy self in the nursery today. For some reason she was very giggly in language as if some of the words were amusing her.

Other than that she enjoyed swimming and was quite cross when it was time to come out. I hope the half-term break goes well for you all and I'll contact you to arrange another meeting in the second half of the term if I may.

A good holiday despite the truly vile weather; trips out were virtually impossible other than when my sister could offer transport but we've been doing lots of crafts.

Adam is a dab hand with arty activities and I've been letting Ruby help with preparing vegetables etc for meals. Most of the time passed pleasantly.

Sunday night was rather different; Ruby's bath and the Halloween party proved too much stimulation and we had major tantrums from her (even a little of her old trying to bang her head/bite her hand behaviour that I thought we'd got her past). Finally calmed her down enough to sleep by 2am.

Monday, 1st November

Aggie - Well, it may have been a short sleep but it did her good. Ruby is sweetness and light today; munched down egg & soldiers and a glass of milk with great gusto. I get the impression she's really looking forward to being back in her regular routine.

Honor here, we're short on staff today (training) and so just a brief note. No problems for Ruby and lots of good work. Could you please send a toilet roll with Ruby tomorrow.

No doubt that Ruby enjoyed being back at

nursery. She's been in a happy, mellow mood with lots of cuddles and kisses for everybody (Ivan not impressed!). In bed asleep for 9.30 and only one change overnight.

Tuesday, 2nd November

Aggie - Ruby in a lovely mood today and with a tremendous appetite; ate a turkey sandwich, banana, cereal and milk. In fact she peeled the banana herself (admittedly she did take a bite out of the skin but spat it back out so no harm done). Also insisted on putting on her own shoes, my efforts to help were stopped and she told me, "Ruby do." I was most impressed.

Honor here, sorry for the mix-up with my message, I should have written that I wanted an EMPTY toilet roll! We all laughed this am when all the children brought us in toilet rolls. We've returned them all and would be grateful if you could send the centres once they're empty. What a silly teacher!

Ruby had a very good day; lots of work and some nice language use.

We're not sure what went wrong but Ruby was asleep for 7.15, awake for 11 and would not go back to sleep until 4.30am.

Wednesday, 3rd November

Aggie - Her parents may be physical wrecks after last night but Ruby is as bright as a button. She has eaten cereal, banana and an orange all washed down with milk. It also appears that she's making a determined grab for bread sticks to take with her presumably in case she feels snacky.

(Adam and I did wonder what you wanted toilet rolls for; a new sort of Christmas decoration?)

Leila here, Ruby, of course, shows no sign of her broken night in fact <u>full</u> of life and energy. She had an excellent individual session with good language use; said "Ready Steady and Go" with a proper gap between them and really tried to get pronunciation correct.

In craft Ruby made a firework (non-explosive!), drew a lovely firework picture, did some cutting and sticking and played with clay.

We were able to stop her eating the clay but she did spread it around I think we're managed to get it all off her clothes and out of her hair.

Horrible, horrible night. Not Ruby's fault at all. You know how terrified she is of barking dogs and with all the early fireworks being set off we seemed to be surrounded by barking and howling dogs the whole night. Did not settle to sleep until 2am and had half-a-dozen wake-ups for changes and noises outside.

Thursday, 4th November

Aggie - What a difference! Ruby awake and out of bed with no problem. She's got a huge appetite today and got washed and dressed in record time and then sat waiting for the bus patiently. No sign of last night's upset (thankfully!)

Honor here, I think we'd all like a dose of Ruby's giggle-juice; she has an amazing sense of humour! I notice lately she seems to be saying more clear words in the middle of her jargon.

Today Ruby has enjoyed painting and

listening to the tape of animal sounds. She had a very good session of individual work and produced some very good and appropriate language. Tomorrow we hope to be taking the children on a trip out in the bus as a treat.

Looking forward to seeing you all tonight.

Well, despite fireworks and barking dogs Ruby has managed to settle to sleep. We think the trip out in the early evening was enough to knock her out. Adam and I are looking forward to some sleep of our own.

Friday, 5th November

Aggie - Ruby in an excellent mood today chatter and play from the moment she woke up. She still has an excellent appetite as well: another big breakfast with cereal, orange, biscuit, grapefruit and anything else she could demand, mooch or steal!

Honor here, we took the children on a trip around the local police station today. The desk sergeant took us all over and introduced all of the officers. He also

organised ink-pads so that the children could take their own fingerprints (see Ruby's included) which they all loved anything messy is a guaranteed winner! Unfortunately once Ruby had finished making her prints she decided to clean her fingers and the sergeant had his uniform tunic used as a wipe. He was very nice about it and laughed saying his grand-children had got much worse things on there on occasion.

We all hope Ruby doesn't have a bad night of things with the fireworks tonight and that the rest of the weekend is easier for you all.

I'm very grateful police uniforms aren't white! She is a little monkey sometimes. Luckily she's been very brave about the whole disruption and coped extremely well this weekend. Generally good sleep until Sunday night when she went to bed at 8pm but was up again in an hour and then awake until 4am. Ho hum.

Monday, 8th November

Aggie - Not sure if it's her broken night but

Ruby has no appetite at all today, however she's cheerful enough and anxious to get to nursery. No sign of a temperature or anything so I hope she's not coming down with something.

Laura here, I'm covering for Honor who's in a meeting today and I have Thelma and Leila as usual to help me. Ruby's appetite seems to be coming back as she asked for another biscuit at snack-time. A good day with no real problems.

I'm sorry I didn't get to meet you on Thursday as our paths didn't cross I've been trying to meet all the parents since taking up this post. Perhaps we could arrange another visit in the new year, if you like?

Yes, Ruby's appetite is back and then some. Ate all before her and demanded more but finally settled for a biscuit and drink of hot chocolate. Not sure if her drink helped but she was asleep for 8 and only needed two changes overnight.

We'd be happy to see you in the new year just suggest a date.

Tuesday, 9th November

Aggie - We're very rushed today so just a quickie to say Ruby's fine- no problems despite our late start. I meant to ask yesterday if you need any more pull-up pants?

Leila here, Ruby in a sunny mood today. She very much enjoyed finger-painting we couldn't keep her away if we tried! Good individual session as well; she loved the bubbles. Ruby also adores the police car siren sound we have on the computer she'll press it over and over if we let her.

We're fine for pull-ups at present Ruby seems to have only a few 'accidents' outside of her regular toileting breaks.

Ruby in a cuddly mood tonight and asked for bed about 8.30, dropping off to sleep very quickly for her. She's obviously enjoyed her day.

Wednesday, 10th November

Aggie - Much better appetite today and Ruby is still feeling better tempered this morning.

We've all noticed she's talking a great deal more in the mornings at one time you were lucky to get a single word from her before breakfast. Now she wakes up and starts demanding things almost as soon as her eyes open; "Milk Coffee", (no, I don't usually give her any as the idea of Ruby on caffeine is just scary) and "Bowl" (which is how she asks for cereal).

Bubbles, by the way, are a prime favourite of Ruby's. When she was younger Ruby used to refuse to be held and would close her eyes and go rigid to avoid contact. Adam and I used to sit and blow bubbles to coax her to sit on our knees we'd sit with her rocking and blowing bubbles for ages. After several months she started coming for the cuddles even when we didn't have any bubbles but I think she still likes bubbles best!

Honor here, Ruby's in a lovely mood and had a busy, happy day. Did hand-painting and collage during the morning, had a nice lunch and then a long individual session with me this afternoon.

She was reluctant to put down her toys for our individual session but did do so

when I coaxed her. Hope you all have a good evening.

Great evening Ruby ate well, enjoyed some games and was in bed for 10.30 with three changes overnight.

Thursday, 11th November

Aggie - A thoroughly happy mood today and Ruby ate a really large breakfast. She seems anxious to get to nursery tonight.

Honor here, all fine here this morning but Ruby not to keen on 'work' first thing, she seemed more interested in games, usually she settles down later in the day. She LOVES swimming. I've noticed lately that Ruby also giggles when I sing a song which ends on a rising inflection.

When asking for things today she used very clearly spoken "home," "more" and also "ready, steady...go." What does she say at home when she wants more?

One bad temper incident with Ruby today when she deliberately bumped her forehead and I wasn't quick enough to

stop her I'm very sorry about that but she seems fine now.

I did hope we'd seen the last of head-banging. Don't apologise, I know how fast Ruby can be and Superwoman couldn't keep up with her in a temper. She's generally been OK but very grumpy for the last half-hour before bed. Asleep by 10 and two changes.

Friday, 12th November

Aggie - Ruby ate a good breakfast today but slopped her drink EVERYWHERE. I do hope she settles down for you.

When Ruby wants more of something she sometimes says "more", but usually just says the name of the thing she wants - "milk" etc. On bad days she goes back to her old habit of sitting and screaming, leaving us to work out what she wants. These days Adam and I refuse to play along and won't give her anything until she stops the tantrum. It's hard on the ears but we think in the long run she has to learn to ask rather than bully people to get her own way.

In fact when she misbehaves we've found the

most effective deterrent is to say, "Unless you stop right now you won't go on the bus (to school) tomorrow. No bus. No school." It's a bit mean but by far the simplest way of stopping her screaming/stamping feet.

Honor here, Ruby has a truly enormous appetite today she ate 3 slices of Cara's birthday cake at snack-time. Not terribly keen on lunch. During the afternoon we had a cookery session where Ruby enjoyed making and then eating instant whip. Seemed to particularly enjoy using the whisk; lots of giggling and laughter when using this.

Today we had our first assembly practice it's our turn next week!! Thank you for all the information, it helps a great deal.

Ruby very disturbed this weekend as her brother Ivan is ill and has been resting on the couch and watching TV. She does hate sharing 'her' TV.

Monday, 15th November

Aggie - In spite of the change to her routine for the weekend Ruby seems to have decided

Monday means we go back to normal and she's back to her happy self. She's been very talkative and made a good breakfast. I hope she stays this good for you.

Honor here, I wasn't here first thing as my youngest was sick all night. Laura covered for me and said Ruby was her usual self when she came in. Thelma and Leila are here so it was work as usual. During the afternoon we went swimming and Ruby enjoyed herself. There were fewer than usual children so Ruby loved it as she got a 40 minute session instead of a 20 minute dip.

Swimming does seem to tire her Ruby came home and was yawning over her tea. She asked for bed by 8 and slept deeply with only two changes.

Tuesday, 16th November

Aggie - Sorry to hear about you youngest's illness, I know how tiring that can be and there are some nasty little bugs around at the moment. Hope they get over things quickly.

Ruby in an excellent mood and made a very

good breakfast. Do you still have enough pull-up pants?

Honor here, Ruby had a slightly different day today. It was the official opening of the nursery extension so we had 20 visitors. She coped <u>very</u> well when the visitors were in the room but afterwards found sitting at group times slightly difficult I expect it was the air of expectation and all of us being in our best dresses etc. I'm glad she slept well last night and hope that continues. Ruby really loved the sensory room this pm particularly pressing all the switches to change sounds and light levels. We had an extra long session because all of the children were so good in the morning. My little girl is better today, thank you for mentioning it.

We aren't having much luck with Ruby using the toilet, do you have any tips?

Ruby ate well and slept fairly well despite another attempted break-in during the night. Two drunken young women were disappointed to find the off-licence closed and prised up a stone to throw through the window and tried to grab what they could. One of them managed to cut herself badly enough that when the police arrived they had to call her an ambulance. Idiots!

Wednesday, 17th November

Aggie - Broken sleep or no Ruby was awake bright and early, in a chatty mood and made a very good breakfast.

I've never had much success with toileting Ruby; she does love the flush and this makes a good reward for when she manages anything. It's not often that she does although she is starting to try to let us know. We have noticed she makes a sort of 'swoosh' noise just before a wee and we try to get her to the toilet. Unfortunately by the time we've got her through two safety gates we're usually in time to clean-up rather than anything else.

She's been talking to the mirror today and making us laugh as she kept saying, "Sit down!"(very stern with a point), "Be good girl", "Sssh", "NO!" etc etc. Ruby also noticed I had burned my arm cooking and kept patting it (ouch!) and saying "ouch" which was nice empathy but still hurt.

Leila here, thank you for all the information you sent today! It really does help us understand her a little more. Ruby has had a lovely day today playing with foot-paint she seemed to enjoy squishing in different paints and cutting out her footprints once they had dried. She also enjoyed having her feet washed and dried afterwards she seemed to think this was another treat in itself.

Once all of her pictures are dried I'll send the nicest home for you and Adam to see how hard she's worked, she's has quite a few pictures to show you.

Sorry to hear your problems with the alarm continue. At least Adam didn't have to intervene this time.

Glad Ruby had such a good day. She came home in a lovely mood but we had a dog-fight outside the flat in the early evening and she's been upset ever since. She's not
had a lot of sleep because every bark or noise wakes her up crying.

Thursday, 18th November

Aggie - The sleep she managed was obviously enough because Ruby woke up in a great mood; noisy but jolly.

She chomped her way through cereal and carrots (not from the same bowl I hasten to add although knowing Ruby she would mix them).

Adam and I loved her pictures and we're not surprised she enjoyed the footprint painting and soaking her feet. When she was very small and wouldn't be held we used to use diluted massage oils and rub her feet to warm and then blow on them to cool them down. The different sensations obviously felt good and we would ask her to look at us to let us know if she wanted us to rub-and-cool again. Every time she glanced we'd repeat until she decided she'd had enough and pushed us away. Gradually the sessions got longer but I think it helped Ruby connect catching somebody's eyes with getting what she wants.

She still loves having her feet rubbed and often asks for this is she is feeling ill or upset but now she likes it as part of being cuddled.

Honor here, Ruby the most <u>responsive</u> she's ever been in hydro she loves the sessions but prefers to do her own thing. However, today she joined in beautifully when requested got out well when asked, quite angelic!!

Not very angelic at home I'm afraid. Tea was thrown all over the floor and we had screaming hysterics. Despite her bad mood we coaxed her to bed by 9.30 so Adam and I could recover. Whew!

Friday, 19th November

Aggie - Recovery only lasted until 5am and then she started again. Poor Adam heroically occupied her whilst I made breakfast. After a bowl of cereal and two oranges Ruby comprehensively used her potty and became her usual cheery self. Half an hour later I had to feed her more cereal and a banana.

When constipated both Ivan and Ruby are ghastly!

Honor here, I've checked with everybody and you're right Ruby hadn't opened her bowels yesterday so she must have been feeling uncomfortable, poor child.

Glad to hear she's sorted herself out. She's been lovely today and made a much better meal today. We even had a near success in using the toilet. Just a little late.

I've been away at the weekend with my sister to visit family but Adam said Ruby was pretty dreadful. Lots of screaming for what she wanted instead of asking and generally a bad mood. I got a very black look when I returned despite bringing her a nice present.

Monday, 22nd November

Aggie - Ruby a little reluctant to wake up at first but then brightened up and ate her breakfast, she became very cheerful. She has been looking at herself in the mirror and singing to her reflection she held quite a long conversation with herself.

Do you need any new pull-up pants yet?

Thelma here, we don't seem to need any pants yet, thanks. Ruby is in a lovely mood today. She has been into everything but work. Nice hydro session

in the afternoon. On Friday we are taking the children out for lunch could you send a little extra for whatever treats she would like and let us know her preferences?

Ruby tired tonight ate her meal, played for an hour and then asked for bed. We kept her going a little longer but she was in bed for 8. Some up-and-downs during the night but she's been fairly mellow for her.

Tuesday, 23rd November

Aggie - Adam and I seem to have this flu that's going around but fortunately neither of the children seem affected. Here's hoping that lasts!

Honor here, Ruby has had a very busy and happy day. We had swimming in the morning and then had a little party for Leila's birthday. Ruby ate well and enjoyed herself with dancing, she seemed especially partial to the party poppers which surprised us considering your problems with fireworks. She adored all the disco music and lights I

think it reminded her of the sensory room.

Ruby very giggly at first, lots of energy (which we frankly couldn't keep up with) and then she suddenly became cuddly and asked for bed. A good night's sleep with two changes.

Wednesday, 24th November

Aggie - Her comfy sleep did her good Ruby's a bundle of energy today and <u>very</u> talkative. She really seems to be trying to communicate rather than just saying words that please her.

I'll send the money for Friday and as to preferences Ruby loves to eat meals 'out' and she will sit and eat nicely. She loves any drink so long as it has lots of ice (she crunches the cubes afterwards) and enjoys fries, not particular about burgers but will eat them.

Honor here, Ruby has had a good day she named the symbols for dinner, drinks and crisps. Also took part in singing '5 Little Ducks' singing "quack, quack ." Liked taking part in activities in the afternoon dough and sticking.

Thank you for the info re meals out, it proved to be very useful. She really does love to crunch ice, doesn't she?

Ruby tired tonight; went to sleep at 8 but was up again at 11 and didn't drop off again until 4.45am.

Thursday, 25th November

Aggie - Sorry, really tired. Ruby fine despite lack of sleep.

Honor here, it sounds as if you're both exhausted. We had swimming in the morning and I kept Ruby in for a 40 minute session- please let me know if it helps with her sleep this evening. We are all thrilled with her response in language said her name at the right time today. Don't forget she has another party tomorrow.

A wonderful, peaceful night; only one change. Thank you SO much!

Friday, 26th November

Aggie - Lots of fruit for breakfast today; she's

in a happy, lively mood and seems excited at the prospect of another party. Very pleased with her new dress! Apparently I'm "nice Mommy nice" today. Hope all goes well and I've given her money to the escort.

Leila here, all fine today. Change in Ruby's purse and she was beautifully behaved. Ate chips, some beefburger and helped herself to yoghurt she really seems to be into yoghurt at the moment. We'll hope to see you all at the Christmas Fayre tomorrow.

I'd say it was a good weekend generally although we had a few blow-ups. Lovely to see everybody at the Fayre on Saturday and wasn't Ruby thrilled to see Father Christmas? On Sunday I succeeded in giving Ruby's hair a little trim without any of the usual kicking and biting. It was a lovely change; I usually dread hairdressing. Best not-birthday present ever.

Monday, 29th November

Aggie - Ruby ate well for breakfast today she had...guess what?...yoghurt! With cereal. Not to mention two oranges and an apple. Somebody was feeling a little peckish!

She's in an excellent mood but ripe for mischief, I'm afraid; she tried picking our cat Fleur up by her tail today. I should mention this isn't intended as cruel on Ruby's part as Fleur purrs throughout and tries to get Ruby to do it again. Only we could have a masochist cat! Truly weird.

Honor here, Ruby settled nicely to puzzles first thing she seems happiest when she gets a clear 10 minutes to carry out her first activity, as if it bookmarks the change from home to school perhaps?

Very responsive in language session said "Go", "Ruby", "more", "How do you do?" and "here I am." Very clear pronunciation. It was also a lovely, lazy session in the pool I hope that will help her sleep tonight!

Thank you for your support on Saturday, we'll find out shortly what funds were raised.

What an amazing night! Ruby in bed asleep by 8 and slept through until 7.30. We had four changes but I don't think she really woke up for these, just surfaced long enough to be washed and changed then drifted off again. Adam and I haven't slept like this in ages.

Tuesday, 30th November

Aggie - Ruby obviously felt the benefit of that good sleep because she's been in a very good mood, although very hungry. A cooked breakfast for her today (I think it helps in this cold weather, don't you?) followed by orange, apple, banana and some hazelnuts that we picked.

When I put her in her new coat today she smiled and patted it saying, "Ruby...coat," very clearly. I think it was a good choice for her.

Honor here, glad to hear the pool session helped, that's great. Ruby found it hard to settle this am but REALLY good in PE this pm. So cooperative: the best she's ever been with us in a session, she did everything asked and seemed to love it all.

Ruby in a calm, happy mood and asleep by 9.30. Only a couple of changes overnight.

Wednesday, 1st December

Aggie - Ruby in a VERY good mood, fits of giggles! When she saw her advent calender she said, "Ruby choc'it pwees." Needless today she got her chocolate drum!

When she came home yesterday there was a small scratch between her eyes; I've given it a wash and it doesn't seem to bother her but please stop her if she starts to pick at it. We're lucky she rarely gets small injuries because she's a devil for pulling off scabs and when anything becomes itchy as it heals she tries to scratch it open again.

Leila here, so far Ruby hasn't touched the scratch as far as any of us can see but we'll keep an eye on her. Pleased to hear it was another good nights sleep I wonder why it is? It's also good to hear she's putting 2-word combinations together herself.

Ruby was cross with me when I asked her to do some work in the morning but then went off by herself and did it! Today she made a robin and did a Xmas painting some beautiful concentration on her work. Are you bringing her to use the

creche next Thursday night so you and and Adam can take Ivan to see the Christmas lights turned on?

Truly amazing. Another happy night, in bed by 10 and good, solid sleep with only a couple of changes.

Thursday, 2nd December

Aggie - Ruby still calm and happy with a hearty appetite; fruit and cereal today. Looking out for the bus as she finished eating. Yes, we do want to use the creche for Ruby, £3 enclosed and completed form; we're taking Ivan to pick his Christmas outfit he says he wants something 'jazzy'. My mind boggles at what he'll pick!

Honor here, thank you for the money and form, we look forward to having Ruby for the evening. We had some lovely chat at the appropriate time in language and a relaxing 40 minutes in swimming. She helped to make her very own Father Christmas in craft this pm

Down from 9.30 to 7am! Barely woke for her

changes. My flabber has never been so ghasted!

Friday, 3rd December

Aggie - Ruby in a lively mood today but less appetite; only wanted fruit for breakfast but playing and singing from the moment she woke up. Her Mickey purse has the £10 and raffle ticket stubs, could you please pass them to the office?

We're putting up the Christmas tree this weekend and hope that this year Ruby will join in.

Thelma here, we're not sure if Ruby had too much fruit but we've had 2 loose bowel movements from Ruby this morning. She didn't want very much lunch and has been a little quiet. Hope this doesn't mean she's poorly.

Good singing practice &language work this am. After lunch had tap-it box and a walk. Hope she's feeling better for the weekend.

We think Ruby has had a touch of the stomach

bug that's going around. Poor appetite and tummy a bit loose on Saturday but seems to be settling. We've kept her in the warm and on a light diet and she seems to be getting back to normal. Leaving the decorations until she feels well enough to help.

Monday, 6th December

Aggie - Ruby grumpy to start with but brightened after her bowl of cereal. I've not given her any fruit to be on the safe side, just milk and crackers. Her temperature is normal and no upset tummy so I think she's over whatever it was.

Honor here, it's been a funny am as half of us were in church practising for the carol concert. Ruby will come up on Wednesday so she's been to the church before Thursday. None of the new children are dressing up this time- it's enough for them to be in a totally new situation. Swimming this pm headmaster was in the pool today which amused the children a great deal (he's practising for his fund-raising swim for the school).

A pretty good night Ruby very excited as we

managed to get the Christmas tree decorated despite - I mean with - her help. She was very hungry when she got home did she not enjoy her lunch? or just making up for lost time from the weekend? Took a long time to settle (11.30) but once she dropped off a good night's sleep.

Tuesday, 7th December

Aggie - Ruby still hungry today; had her usual cereal, fruit and milk and then asked for a sandwich too. Apparently she fancied writing her own comment today and you nearly had crayon scribbles everywhere!

Meant to ask any sign of Ruby's balaclava and gloves? She wore them in during that last cold snap but they never came home (my own fault as I forgot to label them, sorry).

Leila here, whoops! Sorry about her hat & gloves still in her PE bag on the peg! A relaxing day today with no practice. Ruby had individual work, language and a session in the bubble room.

A very disturbed night because there was a lot of noise in the street. Apparently some people are starting their Christmas parties early!

Wednesday, 8th December

Aggie - Ruby in a good mood despite her lack of sleep. She had cereal and 2 bananas today, asked very nicely for the second one. We've noticed she is also singing a lot including a recognisable version of 'Wheels on the Bus'.

Apart from the living room and landing we put up a few decorations in her room last night and she seems thrilled with these.

Honor here, sorry to hear it was a bad night. Slightly disorientated this am as we went to church but Ruby coped well. This pm will be more the regular routine but we are decorating the tree at 2.45.

No ill effects from the changes Ruby in a really nice mood and had a good sleep. Only one change.

Thursday, 9th December

Aggie - Ruby very playful today (tickling the cat who came back for more sigh). She has sneezed a couple of times and sniffs a little but no temperature and a good appetite. I don't think it can be a cold developing as they tend to make her almost stop eating. To be safe I've given her some medicine and extra orange juice.

Honor here, Ruby was <u>very</u> <u>good</u> in church this am. Out to play after lunch then we watched the video of the service and did some work. See you later.

Beautiful evening Ivan's idea of jazzy is surprisingly tasteful he must take after Adam, I prefer a LOT more colour. Ruby, although puzzled by the change in routine, seems to have thoroughly enjoyed herself. A little over-excited so didn't settle until almost 12 but gave us a quiet night.

Friday, 10th December

Aggie - Hm, last night may be having a delayed effect. Ruby in a mood with herself today. She ate well but it was a wrestling match to get her washed and dressed. When I did finally get her into her clothes Ruby threw her unfinished drink all over the floor (and cat; who was quite happy to lick it off since it was milk). After being told off for this she calmed down, ate an orange and became her usual cheerful self.

Leila here, sorry to be brief but we're busy today. Ruby's been fine all day. She did well in singing practice and PE. Made sandwiches this pm. Do tell us if she likes her present!

Ruby LOVED her present but it didn't stop her giving us a hellish weekend. Her sleep pattern is non-existent again and she's only eaten fruit, milk and bread; only nibbled at meals. To be fair this is probably due to her cold.

On Friday, when she got off the bus, there were two scratches under her left eye did she have a fall? I've washed them and applied cream; they seem to be healing nicely as Ruby (luckily) has left them alone.

Monday, 13th December

Aggie - Ruby ate some breakfast today but in a foul mood REALLY grumpy about being washed and dressed. Hope this is just an early morning thing and she cheers up.

Honor here, the scratches appeared at

play time on Friday she spent a long time around one of our profoundly physically handicapped children in his buggy and the feeling is he may have accidentally caught her with one of his uncontrollable physical jerks. As you say Ruby seems to be leaving them alone so I hope they heal quickly.

Ruby has been OK here today although, perhaps, a little quiet (we're not used to that with Ruby!). Making Christmas presents this am and had a language session which went very well. She continues to use 2-word combinations with increasing confidence. Swimming this pm. She does seem to have a little cold her nose appears slightly blocked.]

Would you please send in an orange on Wednesday as we are making Christingles.

Ruby is quite blocked up, only picked at her food and had a slight temperature - although she was in bed for 10pm she remained restless I used some decongestant on her pillow and this seemed to help as she settled quite nicely.

A couple of changes but she settled very quickly each time.

Tuesday, 14th December

Aggie - Ruby in a much better mood today, her temperature is normal and she has eaten a large breakfast. We've been having games today whilst waiting for the bus which she enjoyed a great deal.

Leila here, Ruby fine today. She made an Xmas card this am, played outside and did some PE. Quite quiet this pm she had a relaxing session in the bubble room. Our Christmas party will be held on the 21st of this month and we're asking parents to send in small items to supplement the school meal could we ask you to send party biscuits for all 10 children? Any containers you want returned will need to be labelled as we'll get them all confused I'm afraid. Please can Ruby bring an orange on Wednesday or Thursday for her Christingle?

That sniffle is hanging on poor Ruby has been sniffing and coughing tonight. She didn't settle until gone 12 and was up and down all night.

Wednesday, 15th December

Aggie - Ruby is still snuffly and has sneezed once today but her temperature is normal. I wanted to keep her home to be safe but she cried for her clothes and was such a picture of misery I didn't have the heart to insist. BUT if she is still off-colour/sneezing tomorrow I will keep her home no matter what we want her fit enough to enjoy her Christmas.

Thelma here, Ruby very quiet again especially on the afternoon. We're all trying to get our odds & ends ready for the end of term. We're making Christingles tomorrow.

Gave Ruby medicine and chest rub which seemed to soothe her. She tired very quickly and was down for 8. Lovely, restful sleep with no sneezes/snuffles.

Thursday, 16th December

 has coughed twice I've given her medicine and chest rub just in case. Two bowls of cereal and fruit for breakfast and she's in a lovely mood. Seems very excited. Orange (as requested) in her bag.

Leila here, relaxing day today as we've concentrated on finishing our presents and making the Christingles.

Ruby has been having fun with glitter, I'm afraid, but I did get most of it despite her liberal use of glue. Tomorrow is the Christingle service and all the children seem very excited about this.

Ruby seems clear of sniffles tonight but I'm continuing medicine until I'm sure whatever it is has cleared up completely. Down for 10 and restful sleep (decongestant on her pillow seems to help) with three changes that barely disturbed her.

Friday, 17th December

Aggie - Ruby in such a happy mood today! She's eaten well and I've carried on her medicine although she does appear nearly clear of congestion. Some of the excitement today may be because she has been told that my sister is driving us to Birmingham tonight to visit family over the weekend. Long car rides seems to by Ruby's idea of heaven!

Honor here, we've had a lovely day. It was a super Christingle service this am really beautiful when the lights were put out and all the candle were lit. Ruby <u>very</u> good.

Xmas dinner went wonderfully the tables were all decorated so prettily and I'm writing this as we wait for our puppet show to start. Ruby's christingle is in her bag. We're off to Startleigh on Monday to see Father Christmas. Don't forget no swimming until TUESDAY.

Bit of a scrappy weekend because of the trip but not bad for Ruby she slept for quite a lot of the journey and when awake was smiling and happy. B'ham's Christmas lights are very beautiful and she seemed to enjoy them a lot.

I finally found out what a Christingle is I kept meaning to ask but never got around to it. We had nothing like this in catholic services which seems a shame it's very pretty and I like the symbolism.

Monday, 20th December

Aggie - Ruby is very hyper and giggly - knowing she's going to meet Santa seems to have her all of a twitter but very, VERY happy. She's clear of her sniffle, cough-free and full of mischief she's been taking chocolate decorations from the tree as sneakily as she can. I asked her who had taken them and she told me, "Iyan" which is the closest she can come to saying Ivan's name. He was highly indignant!

Hope all goes well today.

Honor here, thank you so much for the tin of biscuits it was very kind of you both. Ruby has loved her day out. Really enjoyed the grotto looked all around. It was themed on Snow White and the Seven Dwarfs which seemed to delight her, are they a favourite?

Ruby has held her present (a teddy bear) ever since she received him. All the travel a long drive in my car and on the bus will hopefully have tired her out for you tonight.

Such a happy little girl. Ruby wanted bed by 8 and insisted teddy had to go with her. She's never much liked toys in bed with her apart from the little ones she crammed her hands with and they've always tended to be hard. I think she enjoyed cuddling up to something soft for a change.

Tuesday, 21st December

Aggie - Somebody is still tired despite her long sleep yawning over her cereal. She's no longer hyper but still happy so I hope she stays as mellow for the party. A very merry Christmas and happy new year to you. Thank you so much for all your hard work, we really appreciate it. Cards and presents for everybody in the carrier marked with Ruby's name.

Honor here, Ruby has had a very busy, happy day. Swimming in the am went down well and obviously raised an appetite. Ruby tried a lot of everything and enjoyed all the fun of the party particularly party poppers. She seemed particularly taken with the disco and lights although at times she was sticking

her fingers in her ears and hunching up, something we rarely see these days. Not that I blame her there were times I felt like doing the same!

All of us say 'thank you' for our beautiful presents and hope you have a wonderful Christmas and a **PEACEFUL** new year.
See you in January!

****

Last day of the Autumn Term

Dear All,

well the end of another term in the nursery, six new children have joined us and settled well. It's now hard to imagine life without them. Leonard leaves us today and joins the infant class in January. We've enjoyed having him and wish him every success in his new class. After Christmas Stevie will be full time and John is coming on Thursday as well as his other days. A new boy called Gerry is joining us on Wednesday, Thursday and Friday.

Linda, Thelma, Leila and I would like to thank you all for our cards and presents. We've been thoroughly spoilt and called "The girls" more than once it makes us feel 20 years younger!

Next term starts on Thursday, 6th Jan. Our theme for the term will be teddies bears and sounds. Please cut out any pictures of teddy's you see.

With very best wishes to you all,

Happy Christmas,

Honor, Laura, Thelma and Leila

****

A brilliant Christmas, Ruby has enjoyed every minute of it. A lot of clear language and about twenty new words (Santa, reindeer, present etc). We have had a bit of wallpaper stripping but this appears to have stopped again and (fortunately) no return to gouging at the plaster. A good job because Adam was fed up of filling holes and painting!

Ruby has eaten like a horse! Adam & I have

had this miserable flu throughout the holiday but both of the children escaped it mercifully. In all a successful break.

****

<u>Thursday, 6th January</u>

Aggie - Ruby woke up today very happy and excited. She's eaten well and keeps saying, "School, school", so we take it she's anxious to see you all!

Amongst the teddy items I'm sending are some teddy decal soaps which I thought it might be nice for the children to use.

Honor here, so glad Xmas went well but sorry to hear you both were so poorly. Thank you very much for all the teddy things really super.

Next week can Ruby bring in her teddy bear to keep here for a while. She's found sitting at group times quite difficult today. I think it's just taking her a little time to get back into our routine. She loved swimming a lovely long session to help her keep calm.

Calmer this pm obviously remembered what it was all about and fell back into her usual afternoon routine. Ate 2 biscuits before coming home Christmas seems to have perked up her appetite.

Ruby happy when she arrived home, ate well and asleep for 11.30. Good, solid sleep and only one change.

Friday, 7th January

Aggie - The happy mood continued when she woke. Ate well, talked and sang a great deal while waiting for bus.

Leila here, Ruby has had a good day especially at PE. Enjoyed the tap-it box and the musical TV we've found. Hope you have a good weekend.

It was a fairly good weekend but Ruby's sleep pattern is disrupted again. However, I've managed to trim her fringe at last and not one bite!

Monday, 10th January

Aggie - Ruby very upset when she woke up

crying and shaking, we're not sure why. Maybe a bad dream? After coaxing and cuddles she cheered up and ate well.

Honor here, Ruby all fine once she got to nursery. She's had a very good day. Enjoyed swimming- very cooperative had a 40 minute session. Said "Teddy" a few times. Hope she sleeps better tonight.

When asked Ruby took off and hung up her hat and coat a first! She slept well but in shifts. Dropped off and had to be put to bed 4.30pm to 7.30pm and then down again 3.30 am to 7am. She wasn't upset exactly but agitated and needed a lot of soothing.

Tuesday, 11th January

Aggie - Ruby very hungry today ate well but keeps on picking. She seems unaffected by her disturbed night, in fact revoltingly cheerful! I suspect Ruby realises we're both tired because she's been very affectionate.

Leila here, a good morning joined in singing "Roly poly." We forgot to tell you Ruby said "splash, splash"yesterday.

Enjoyed cutting-and-sticking in am. Had bubble room this afternoon.

Sleep still disrupted down for 12.30, awake by 5am and back to sleep for 6.30am.

<u>Wednesday, 12th January</u>

Aggie - Ruby super difficult today; did not want to get washed/dressed/eat breakfast. Eventually coaxing paid off but she really had to be jollied along every step of the way.

Adam and I cannot identify any reason for this bad patch (we haven't made any changes recently) and we're putting it down to a delayed reaction to the Christmas excitement.

Honor here, sorry to hear Ruby's out of sorts. Not too bad here into tipping things out at present. Wanted a toy dog before individual work but coped when she couldn't have it and had to work first. She loves the Roly Poly song!

Calm night and asleep for 10pm with one a couple of changes. We're crossing our fingers that whatever it was upsetting her is past.

Thursday, 13th January

Aggie - Maybe it's over Ruby a lot happier today, eating like a horse (how unusual!). She's been chattering the whole time and when I dressed her today she spontaneously named several items.

Honor here, Ruby in good form and wanted lots of cuddles in the hydro pool joined in beautifully with the others. A party in the pm for Gerry who only started yesterday lots of food which Ruby loved!

Rather full when she came home so I held tea back for an hour and then she ate with her usual gusto (where does she put it?). Asleep for 10 and slept well.

Friday, 14th January

Aggie - Ruby very happy today and an enormous appetite. I actually got kissed when I gave her breakfast! It may be cupboard love but I'll take what I can get.

Honor here, an odd incident mid-way through this am she went very quiet in

PE and crouched down for a while. Seemed tearful and didn't know how to sort herself out, didn't really want a cuddle. Went into class and had a drink of water and then seemed OK. We didn't know if she stood on something with her bare feet (couldn't see anything) or had a tummy-ache.

Fine later on but sat more quiet and still than usual at tap-it box time she's generally up-and-down wanting her go. Ate lots of crisps at 2.45. Hope everything's OK.

Not a bad weekend although we've had some problems and quite a few tantrums. Appetite all over the place; picking at meals and demanding milk all the while. No obvious sign of what is bothering her. She's got a small spot on her right upper shin that looks nasty (and she keeps scratching and picking) but I've treated with antiseptic and we're keeping her hands away from it so that should settle down.

Monday, 17th January

Aggie - Ruby in a happy mood; more appetite and lots of cuddles. I did have 2 full pots today (sorry to be so graphic) so perhaps she was a little constipated. Certainly a lot brighter now.

Thelma here, no swimming as the boiler went out at the weekend and it was too cold. We had singing and went for a walk instead this afternoon. Ruby was fine with the change and seemed to like her walk in the fresh air. Could you please send any empty boxes you have for craft-work on Friday.

Ruby fairly tired down for 10 but rather disturbed and niggly, making moaning noises even when asleep.

Tuesday, 18th January

Aggie - Ruby in a terrible mood to start with; spot on her leg inflamed and obviously sore. Adam bravely popped it for her and I treated with antiseptic. She cheered up a lot afterwards ate and drank as usual. Very excited by her new shoes, took them off and put them on several times and paraded around in front of the mirror trying to see how they looked.

Leila here, we're short of staff today due to illness. No problems, more tomorrow.

Sorry to hear about illness Ruby fine and slept well, only one change.

Wednesday, 19th January

Aggie - Sweetness and light today; she's been smiles from the first time her eyes opened. Hope staff are feeling better and that her sunny mood lasts.

Honor here, we're only down one staff member today. All fine this am Ruby gave very good responses to symbols at key times of day (dinner & home) says them very clearly and gets us organised! I'm in a different room Thursday & Friday Laura in nursery plus rest of team.

Ruby had a good night but some disruption with dogs barking. No appetite never a good sign. I hope she's not coming down with what the staff had.

Thursday, 20th January

Aggie - Ruby awake for 6.30am and very

happy; playful and very hungry. Cereal, two yoghurts, fruit and fruit juice. Lots of talking and singing as well. She seems to be over whatever it was very quickly.

Could you please keep an eye out for the blue trousers Ruby wore last Friday. She came home in tracksuit bottoms so I assume needed changing?

Honor here, Ruby wore pink trousers which she got wet- we've washed them. Could these be the ones? Hydro today, cutting, individual work am with singing and games for pm.

Good night's sleep despite barking dogs!

Friday, 21st January

Aggie - Ruby woke in a grumpy mood but cheered up after breakfast. Yes, those are Ruby's pink trousers (I hadn't even noticed they were missing!). Now I just have to figure out what I've done with the blue ones! I don't know where my head is recently. This is probably something to do with poor Ivan having nightmares and Adam and I being up and down comforting him. Hope the boxes are suitable.

Honor here, many thanks for the boxes, they're quite suitable. A good day for Ruby today with some nice interaction. Hope poor Ivan has a better night and the two of you get some more sleep! Enjoy the weekend.

Not really a bad weekend but VERY tiring. Ruby sleeping and eating but in a tormenting mood very naughty but giggling and treating it all as a joke. In some ways that's worse than her tantrums - I feel horrible if I shout at her for being naughty but she makes just as much mess as when she's in a temper.

Monday, 24th January

Aggie - A nice smile when she woke up but hell-on-wheels from then on. Ruby has been going from one lot of mischief to another and thoroughly enjoying herself. Managed to get cereal, yoghurt, milk and vitamins down her despite being smeared with soggy cereal and having her first drink deliberately thrown on me with a happy little smile.

Just in case she does similar things in the nursery please note that if she is told off Ruby will repeat the behaviour over and over. I usually tell her that she is acting like a silly baby and to act like the big girl she is. This, coupled with a total refusal to lose your temper will probably frustrate her and cause a tantrum but it will eventually make her stop and calm down. She then usually becomes very affectionate I'm not sure why but that's a pretty regular pattern with her.

Honor here, thanks for the info re playing up she's been OK this am apart from kicking someone because she wanted their toy. Ruby's very interested in the new nursery toys particularly a wind-up 'Old McDonald' with interchangeable moveable parts.

She coped with a change in routine well today as we went into the hall to do some science I was really pleased with the way she coped. Enjoyed swimming in pm and had long session.

Homework!! Ruby needs to learn 'Old McDonald' for assembly using Makaton

signs. We're just doing duck, sheep and cow verses if you could practice those with her for next week.

My goodness I didn't expect homework in the nursery! Of course I'll go through it with her, Old Mac is one of her favourites and we sing it fairly regularly so I'm usedto the signs. Ruby's a lot better tonight with good appetite and behaviour. Down for 10 and only a couple of changes. I could get used to this!

Tuesday, 25th January

Aggie - Ruby in a really nice mood today with amazing appetite; cereal, 2 bananas, grapes, part of a baby grapefruit and a strawberry mousse. It seems to have suited her because she's in a fabulous mood very happy and playful. Adam and I have heard about 20 clear, appropriate word uses in about two hours everything from "baby", "teddy" to "breakfast" and "gorgeous." Even a few familiar phrases like "clothes on" and "go school." We'll see you later.

Honor here, thank you both for supporting the coffee am I'm sorry I didn't see you both but we had a

particularly busy am. Ruby was really good but some of the others were a handful! Great to hear about all that language.

A terrible night Ruby asleep between 10pm to 12.30 then awake until 4.30am.

Wednesday, 26th January

Honor here, I hope you've caught up with your sleep today. Apart from one upset when Ruby managed to leave the room with a 'mickey' which she then wouldn't put down for language work she's had a really good day. Worked very well when asked. Hope you have a better night.

Ruby asleep for 8.30. Thanks be.

Thursday, 27th January

Aggie - Sorry for yesterday's lack of comment, both of us so tired we stumbled through the morning routine on automatic pilot. We've caught up now and feel much better. Ruby full of beans today and a bit mischievous.

Leila here, good to hear you've both got some rest. Ruby calmer by the time she reached nursery and had a good day. Swimming in the am which she enjoyed and a nice walk out on a rare sunny afternoon.

Yet another good night. The fresh air obviously worked so we're hoping for more good weather!

Friday, 28th January

Aggie - Ruby in a very nice mood today healthy appetite, talking, singing and lots of cuddles. Decided she wanted to look and play with the photo-book today.

Honor here, Ruby far more willing to come in and work in the am (before 9.45) sits at the tables and usually does what's asked. Previously she liked to settle into school in her own way.

She did PE today but again asked to be picked up and we are wondering if she finds the floor too cold with bare feet. I know she isn't keen on pumps but I think

**it may be worthwhile to try her again.
Hope you have a good weekend.**

A good weekend. We took a trip into town on Saturday and picked up some flowery pumps that Ruby found acceptable. Perhaps that will help. Her sleep is a lot better at the moment.

Monday, 31st January

Aggie - My apologies for Ruby's state she was in a lovely mood until the people over the road went out and left their dog howling and barking on the step (yes, the same ones who own the motorcycle we WISH would get stolen). We had thirty minutes of screaming hysterics before it shut up and we could calm her down once Ruby's gone I'll have a word with them about the blasted thing.

I'll be at the school for 9.45 to attend Ruby's dental check-up, especially because after this upset she may be difficult to handle.

Honor here, as you saw yourself Ruby was fine by the time she got to nursery and has continued that way for the rest of the am. We've started to try individual

sensory work with her and hope to have her transitioned to this after Easter. A party for Lois the pm.

We were practising for our assembly and Ruby LOVED dressing up as a chick and she's a brilliant chick carries out all the movements perfectly. Thank you for the coaching!

You're welcome. I'm just glad everything was OK and the check-up went so well. A good night when Ruby got home but she was being a terrible tease about going to sleep. Kept asking for bed and then getting up again and giggling about it!

Tuesday, 1st February

Aggie - A much more happy morning today as no barking dog (both Adam and I had a word with the owners!). She really enjoys doing the assembly song we had several impromptu performances today.

Laura here, a good am Ruby comes really nicely and takes your hand when asked to come and do an activity. We watched a video one of the mainstream mum's

took of the nursery Ruby was amused to see herself. Honor was on non-contact time today so I'm standing in for her. Otherwise Ruby had a busy, happy day with no problems.

A good night; quite a lot of dog and car noise but Ruby went down for 10pm anyway. Not often that happens!

Wednesday, 2nd February

Aggie - Ruby woke up singing at 6am today so I'm guessing she enjoyed her sleep. Very hungry- yoghurt, fruit, juice and milk disappeared as if by magic.

She's also very cuddly. Sat on my knee & Adam's singing and stroking our faces and hair. Whilst she was doing this to me I noticed her right forefinger knuckle seems slightly bruised & scraped. Did she catch this on something? I'm just concerned it looks a little like the injuries she used to cause herself with self-biting and we don't want her going back to that! Her poor hands used to get in a state unless we watched her like hawks.

Adam and I have racked our brains and we can't think of anything she's done at home (other than by chewing) that could cause it. I've dabbed on some witch-hazel but Ruby is totally indifferent more interested in her second yoghurt.

Honor here, no, none of us have seen any biting but she was playing outside (when we briefly had the sun) in the afternoon so it may have happened then. We'll keep an eye on her just in case thank you for the warning.

Ruby enjoyed looking at the farm display sits at the table really looking and examining it all. In love with one of the chicks. She'll need her yellow jumper for our assembly next Friday. She was very good this pm listening to the local school perform their percussion music for us.

She needs more pull-ups, please. Are you coming to the talk tonight?

Thursday, 3rd February

Aggie - Very lively today, talking the whole time. She ate very well. I'm sending all the pull-ups I have right now and I'll send a full pack tomorrow.

Finally decided not to attend the talk as I'm afraid I'm coughing everywhere right now - I didn't want to disrupt everybody or risk giving them whatever form of the dreaded lurgy I've managed to catch now!

Honor here, Ruby's had a happy day. Hydro this am and work & playing with clay in the pm.

Sorry you had to miss the talk (it was very good) and hope your cough clears up soon. You're not having much luck with your health right now, are you? Young children always seem to catch everything and then pass it on to poor mummy I know my children have frequently done it to me!

An appalling night. Ruby very quiet but seemed happy enough; went to sleep about 9 and then up again and very disturbed. Sick twice and took a lot of cleaning and calming.

Wednesday, 9th February

Aggie - Ruby finally seems to have cleared whatever it was out of her system. No temperature, normal potty and a good appetite once more. She seems very happy and relaxed but anxious to get back to school (I haven't been very popular for keeping her off - afraid I'm back to "bad Mommy!" again). If she should show any recurrence of symptoms please call my sister (Rebecca)'s number and she will drive me to pick her up.

By the way, we've received a latter from the Social services (Care Manager for Children with Special Needs) inviting us to let her know of any services/information that would be useful to Ruby. Is there anything you would recommend we have no idea what's available and the letter contains no guidance about what they can provide. I can't think what else could be done for Ruby or ourselves (unless somebody could magically gift us with the ability to go without sleep. That'd be useful) but you have much more experience of what special needs children require.

Adam and I have a bit of a crisis on attending the assembly it turns out Ivan is performing in his own assembly and at least one of us has to be there so I'll attend but Adam will go to Ivan's. Sorry about that

Honor here, lovely to have Ruby back again. We've all given her lots of encouragement and attention to welcome her back and Ruby seems to thrive on being the focus of the nursery. She came back to a lively assembly 'space' music which fascinated her. After assembly we had drinks and PE followed by practice for our own assembly on Friday. Lunch, out to play, tap-it box and cooking & eating egg sandwiches. Ruby ate the bread but left the eggs.

There's no crisis with assembly as this time parents don't come to ours I'm sorry you didn't realise that. The assembly will be videoed and you are welcome to borrow it. Ruby just LOVES being a chick! She's full of smiles and giggles as she performs the song.

I can't think of anything that she needs right now but she almost certainly will at some point. Have you got your own care manager?

Ruby quite tired but very happy when she got home. Down for 10 and slept well.

Thursday, 10th February

Aggie - Ruby a little grouchy today first thing but cheered after breakfast. Her normal self when waiting for the bus.

No, we've not been assigned anybody that we know of after Ruby's assessment we had a student social worker assigned to us briefly but after a couple of visits everything went quiet.

THANK you for the news about Friday; we were feeling dreadfully guilty at the idea of only one of us going to Ivan's assembly when we usually both manage to be there for Ruby's school events. Poor old Ivan already misses out on time with Mom & Dad because we have to focus so much on Ruby's needs thank heavens for my family because Nanny, Grandad and Auntie are always there to make sure he gets support with his needs if we're not available. We're lucky they live so close by.

Laura here, some staff off ill. Very busy today, Ruby's had no problems. Please remember to send Ruby's yellow jumper with her for the assembly.

You should have been told you are entitled to a care manager of your own if you ever need one. Quite a few of our families have them.

A little disturbed last night probably the change in routine with people being ill. Down for 11 but awake between 3am and 4am with lots of changes the rest of the time.

Friday, 11th February

Aggie - Ruby seems a bit subdued today but not cross. She has been slightly playful but generally rather 'dreamy'. Hope everything goes well at assembly. Her yellow jumper and white tights are in bag with a spare pair in case of accidents.

Honor here, we pulled in some extra helpers for assembly and I think it went really well. Ruby behaved beautifully throughout she didn't want to wear her

costume but looked fine in her jumper and tights. I'll send the video home when it's available. Otherwise a good day with excellent tap-it box in pm.

Sounds as if Ruby had a fine time and certainly came home in a lovely mood ate well and went to bed at 9. No barking dogs for a change so she got some good quality sleep.

Ivan performed brilliantly in his assembly not only playing an instrument but gave one of the readings with good reading (which he can struggle with when reading aloud) and a nice strong voice. He was so grown-up and we're glad both of us could be there to see him.

The rest of the weekend has been strange more disrupted sleep and Ruby keeps coming out in red blotches that appear suddenly and go just as quickly. We think it's an allergy but I've not worked out what is causing it. No temperature, appetite fine and her mood is generally just lack of sleep and itchy, mystery blotches.

Monday, 14th February

Aggie - Just a few blotches today and no

temperature or upset tummy so I'm risking sending her but don't hesitate to call if there are any problems. I've given her an oatmeal bath this morning which seems to have soothed her skin down and I've kept her to simple cereal and milk. The blotches don't seem to annoy Ruby; she's puzzled by them but otherwise not bothered, in fact in a very happy mood; cuddles and kisses all round. Poor Ivan!

We've been talking about the care manager issue to our knowledge we do not have one, nor a social worker. We were surprised to even get a letter apart from the special safety gate the occupational therapist supplied their attitude seems to have been we were fine and just to get on with it. It must have been 18 months or more since we last heard from them.

Our health visitor is the same turns up once every 6 months, chats for about an hour and then fades out again. I suppose it's reassuring that we're getting things right but it does make you wonder what these people are for. We fill in their forms, answer their sometimes extremely personal questions, have to allow

Ruby's routine to be disrupted by their visits (which she hates) and what does the poor child get out of it? Nada.

Honor here, Ruby had a fantastic day today making 3 symbol sentences all by herself at certain times of day eg "we eat dinner", "we go PE" and "we go swimming." She finds the symbols she wants by herself and puts them in the correct order. After lunch she made "we go PE" and started to undress I think she was trying to tell me something. Blotches up and down all day some appear circular but go down too quickly to be certain.

Thanks for all your information re care manager etc. It does appear that you're not really getting any support with Ruby. You should have been assigned a social worker I'm fairly certain and they (together with your health visitor) are there to let you know about services and help with any problems. I do know some parents have said it sometimes takes a long time getting a permanent social worker assigned but 18 months sounds a long time.

A very good night Ruby ate well, in a lovely mood and the blotches seem to have finally disappeared! Still no clue what cause them or why they've gone away. Asleep for 9pm and no barking dogs for a change so she had a good quality nights rest.

Tuesday, 15th February

Aggie - Ruby very happy and quite peckish to day. We're thrilled to hear about the symbol sentences it's brilliant the way Ruby just suddenly springs things like this on everybody.

I can't say I'm surprised about her trying to push you into extra PE, she does like her own way. A few weeks back she was playing with us on the evening and suddenly said,"choc'lit." When I told her we didn't have any in Ruby picked up her things saying, "clothes. Shop. Choc'lit. NOW!" We thought it such an appropriate use of language to get what she wanted I dressed her and took her downstairs to the shop to buy her some sweets. Ruby was very smug!

As regards care managers and all the other social services stuff, although Adam and I moan about being left to cope on our own we're both well aware there are lots of people in far worse situations. It's just irritating to us that it feels as if we're expected to drop everything when we're dealing with Ruby or lose precious catch-up time for sleep to fill in forms, attend meeting or appointments and rattle out the same information over and over again for nothing.

When Ruby initially went through assessment we repeated ourselves so many times I felt like making a recording and playing it back when asked to tell them everything again. I don't even remember how many forms we had to fill in. It was almost a relief when they shut up and left us alone except then you're left wondering what you did it all for? We didn't need the social services to tell us we were doing the right things for Ruby she made it quite clear if she was happy or not herself.

Honor here, everything fine today, Ruby worked well and took part in everything very well. One odd thing was that she came up with a funny blister on her hand and then it went down again Laura couldn't believe it as she thought Ruby

had burnt herself somehow and we'd been checking the radiators.

I do understand how frustrating it can be when you're already so busy and tired, especially when Ruby is happy and doing so well. I've had other parents express almost exactly the same thoughts. All I can say is to remind people of what it takes to care for somebody with Ruby's needs you've quite enough on your plates without any extra pressure.

Thank you for your response. Sorry to climb on my soap-box! No sign of any blisters she does seem to be having some skin problems right now. We used to have a strange thing when she was younger where seams would rub her skin the start of her stripping off so much. I used to have to unpick seams and hand-sew them flat to stop it happening. Hope that's not starting up again! Ruby in a very good mood; happy and relaxed. A lovely, calm night and good sleep.

Wednesday, 16th February

Aggie - Ruby in a really good mood; full of

giggles and mischief. Obviously still remembering Friday as she keeps singing Old Mac and her own version of the Chick song. Afraid I'm still coughing and sneezing I do hope this clears up before the half-term.

Thelma here, Ruby's worked hard all day and did some good cutting. A little more than we wanted actually she decided to try trimming the end of my skirt for me but luckily they're plastic scissors so no harm done. I don't think I've got the legs for a mini-skirt!

Oh, she is a monkey, isn't she? Glad to hear no damage done and I hope you told her off I know she knows better than that. Obviously mischief is tiring because she was yawning over her tea and in bed by 8.30. A very good night with nice deep sleep, only a couple of changes.

Thursday, 17th February

Aggie - Cuddly today and lots of singing. She ate breakfast very nicely and waited very patiently for the bus today.

Honor here, Ruby's had a good day. Lots

of good work and she's working hard on making symbol sentences. Definitely showing more independence and confidence in using language.

My she was ratty when she got home. We suspect Ruby was constipated because she used her pot and became a different person smiles and fun again. A good evening and she went to sleep around 10; we were smiling to ourselves listening to her sing the chick song as she dropped off.

Friday, 18th February

Aggie - A calm, dreamy mood today but she only picked at breakfast so she may make up for it at lunch. Hope everybody has a good half-term.

Leila here, everybody having an easy day today. Ruby did some good language work am and lots of painting, outside play and a walk pm. She's been very playful and smiling but didn't seem particularly hungry. Hope things go well for her break.

A good holiday. Ruby making more effort to interact with others rather than just 'doing her own thing' but quickly tires if she's not the centre of attention. We've had some lovely artwork over the holiday and Adam had Ruby and Ivan playing with papier-mache. They made some lovely bowls and shapes but I was less fond of what Ruby did to her clothes not to mention her hair!

Monday, 28th February

Aggie - Ruby awake bright and early and in a wonderful mood. When reminded she was going to school she said, "swimming...Ruby" and laughed. Lovely appetite and wanting lots of games.

Tuesday, 1st March

Aggie - Talk about 'spot the deliberate mistake'! I carefully made a note in the diary that the children went back on different days then forgot to check the diary!

Never mind. Once we realised my mistake, with yesterday's lovely weather, my sister took the two of us for a drive. Then Adam and I walked Ruby into town and we went shopping.

Ruby loved having Mum & Dad to herself, especially with ice-cream too! When we got home she was so tired we had an afternoon nap (it's been a LONG time since we had one of those!). Although that meant a late night it was good, solid sleep once she finally dropped off.

Awake bright and early today and full of mischief. When I gave her breakfast and I told her she was going to school she gave me this deeply sceptical look.

I said, "Mommy made a mistake yesterday. She's a stupid Mommy sometimes.""Yes Ruby said clearly and grinned.

I must mention that Ruby is so independent when she goes in the car now that once she is fastened in the back-seat she no longer insists on having a grown-up with her.   Yesterday I sat in the front and she had a great time being a 'big girl'.

Honor here, glad to hear Ruby coped so well with your false start to the half-term. Lovely to see all the children back again today. Ruby settled in well looked for Mickey's on arrival LOVED the new

computer & programmes I've learnt to work over the break- obviously appreciated the good graphics! Most definitely did the sound effects.

She got us all organised with drinks & dinner at the right time. PE & bubble room this pm.

Ruby very excited and happy when she got home; quite hyper early evening and then playful the rest of time. She did not settle until 2am but then good, solid sleep once she was settled.

Wednesday, 2nd March

Aggie - Ruby a little tired today (who isn't?) but very happy; ate well. Very playful and cuddly.

Honor here, what a time to go to bed! Sorry, we obviously didn't work her hard enough yesterday. Still loves the new computer programme. Ruby hears if I change the programme and comes rushing over to watch.

Not your fault if Ruby's in 'batteries not included' mode but she made up for it tonight anyway. Down for 9.30 and a wonderful night's rest.

Thursday, 3rd   March

Aggie - Ruby didn't wake up until 8! In a really nice mood- dreamy but cuddly, but not much appetite. I sprained my ankle on our stairs yesterday (slipped on a sock when carrying washing and feel like an idiot) and Ruby think my hobbling is most amusing!

Leila here, ouch! Hope the ankle feels better soon Ruby's hard enough to catch with both feet working properly. Ruby had a good swim this am. Very good with individual work in pm using lots of words and new word combinations.

Nice mood when she came home. Up until late (12) but nice, solid sleep when she finally went to sleep.

Friday, 4th March

Aggie - Ruby very happy today; woke up in a

lovely mood. Had a good breakfast and enjoyed lots of cuddles.

Honor here, today- before PE Ruby got out the symbol for 'we' and then looked for symbol saying 'PE' I gave her that one and said, "Get 'go', Ruby." She went and got it, brilliant! Put them all in the right order. Hope you have a good weekend.

We're thrilled about her use of symbols, hope she tries some more!

A very good weekend. Some broken sleep but Ivan having a break with my parents and sister (so he gets to be the centre of attention for a while) and Ruby loved having Mom & Dad to herself.

Monday, 7th March

Aggie - Lovely, happy mood today; giggles and cuddles all the while, ate a good breakfast. Good sitting and very patient waiting for bus.

Ruby insisted on a 'dress' today so I've bundled her up with tights & a warm cardigan to make sure she doesn't get cold. Sorry about the buttons on dress/cardigan I'll see for future if I can adapt them with snappers or velcro.

Being hopeful I'm sorting out Ruby's warm weather clothes right now lots of shorts and cute dresses. Now all we need is the weather!

Honor here, Ruby all fine today. Enjoyed her symbol work & requesting more very consistently. Swimming in the PM. We all liked her 'summer' outfit she looked so pretty!

Great night; my sister took us out for a drive at 8 and we visited Devil's Point. Ruby almost fell asleep eating an ice-cream and had to be carried to bed. Lovely, solid and relaxed sleep

Tuesday, 8th   March

Aggie - Ruby woke up in a great mood; ate a good breakfast but then became mischievous. Lots of throwing and spilling things and when told off we had full-blown hysterics. Calmed her down and she's seems more settled now.

Leila here, Ruby painted a tree and enjoyed computer this am. Sat very nicely for number rhymes and songs,

played with beanbags and passed it nicely around the circle. Bubble room in the pm.

I've popped the tape of assembly in her swimming bag for both of you to watch.

A good night; whole family got together to watch Ruby's video and she LOVED seeing herself on TV. We had another late evening ride and Ruby down for 10.30 with good sleep, couple of changes.

Wednesday, 9th March

Aggie - Happy mood today, very cuddly but so vague about washing, dressing and eating it took twice as long as usual. Thank you for the video my parents were fascinated to see her taking part in an assembly, I gather things were very different for people with Ruby's needs in their day. We were all amazed at how well-behaved Ruby was - she's come a long way since starting Upham nursery.

Honor here, so glad you all enjoyed the video; Ruby was very good wasn't she? Funnily enough she didn't want to wear

the hat & wings on the day even after having loved doing so before. It didn't matter, she really wanted to take part and accepted her 'props' as part of that.

Thelma brought in a few different toys for us today- Ruby really likes the water pillow and would like to take it everywhere with her BUT very good at putting it back in just the right place before doing something else. I'm off to do home visits this pm so Laura in charge with rest of team.

Wonderful night; we had Chinese from a new take-away & Ruby tasted a bit of everything (although as usual loved rice the best). That with meringue nests topped by chocolate ice-cream ensured a happy Ruby. Asleep for about 10.30, only one change.

Thursday, 10th March

Aggie - Ruby awake bright and early full of beans. Lots of laughing and cuddles. Tried a new breakfast today, strawberry muesli; after some initial mistrust Ruby polished off a bowl and demanded a couple of yoghurts.

Adam and I have noticed a lot more 2-word combinations recently - "good mor'ing","calm down" etc. Have you noticed this?

Honor here, busy day today, we have two families visiting about possible new children for September. Ruby had painting & cutting, language in am and swimming in pm. No problems. We have noticed changes in her language more tomorrow.

Lively night; Ruby initially tired and down early but woke up again at 3am. Very over-the-top; alternating between giggles and tears. We didn't get her down again until 5.30am.

Friday, 11th March

Aggie - Late start for Ruby today (as you can imagine after her disturbed night); she's somewhat glassy-eyed. She's eaten well but remains pretty vague and withdrawn. Enjoys a cuddle if asked but snuggles in and starts yawning.

Honor here, time for comments today! We have noticed more 2-word combinations - "want more" is a

favourite when doing her symbol work! She seems to be more awake now. PE this am, out to play after lunch. Finished the day with jelly we made yesterday and chocolate biscuits Ruby loved it!

For tap-it box she sits nicely now and only chooses one toy at picking time (she used to find it hard to pick just one!). Have a good weekend. Don't forget -training day on Monday, no nursery until Tuesday

Lively weekend; some sleep disruption and appetite all over the place. Picking meals one sitting and then gorging at others.

We're pleased to hear you've all noticed these new combinations (and not at all surprised about "want more!. Adam and I try to reinforce her language use and lavish praise when she uses it.

Managed to take Ruby to Mass with Ivan and she had a great time. Loved the singing and candles but became bored when we reached Homily so she decided to start singing again. I used cuddles and outright bribery (sugar-free mints) to keep Ruby calm you'd have been proud of her, I know I was. Ivan remarked that she was better behaved than many of the other children. For Ivan to be complimentary she must have been positively angelic!

Tuesday, 15th March

Aggie - Ruby in a lively mood today; a little aggressive, suddenly started pulling my hair as I washed and dressed her. Freed myself, told her off and gave her a lots of breakfast and cuddles until she was better tempered.

Honor here, last thing yesterday Ruby said, "we go home" in response to being shown the symbol sentence 3 words together!

Sat beautifully for number songs & rhymes this am. Went shopping for card & flowers this pm one of our helpers has a birthday tomorrow. Does Ruby ever cry very quietly if she gets cold? She got upset while out but cheered up with some chocolate buttons. Rather cross towards home-time. Wonder if she needs her bowels open.

Spot on! Horrendous night; tears, tantrums and general carrying-on. Didn't go to sleep until 2.30am and up again at 6.

Wednesday, 16th March

Aggie - Ruby appears much happier now her bowels are sorted. Appetite back to normal and her cuddly self again. Meant to say thanks for sending a copy of Ruby's programme; it's so exciting for Adam and I to see all the new things she's doing now. We'll do our best to get the pictures you asked for to put in her folder. Do wish 'happy birthday' to your helper although it's a rotten weather day for any celebration.

Honor here, Ruby did really well today with new symbols - "teddy", "drink", "dolly" and "eat"- she gave an excellent response. She's in a much happier mood today presently roaring with laughter at a video of some characters in a garden.

Bit of a roughish night Ruby rather grumpy and unwilling to settle. We've had a few tantrums because of barking dogs.

Thursday, 17th March

Aggie - All better today; Ruby woke up smiling and singing. Ate a good breakfast and then mugged Adam for extra yoghurt.

I made the mistake of catching a tangle in her hair today with the brush & got kicked.   When I yelped she said, "ouch" and gave me a kiss.

Leila here, all fine today Ruby enjoyed swimming after she'd put Mickey down. Unfortunately she came down down to the pool with him & had to go back and return him but she managed. Sitting really well in the group session after lunch waiting for her turn & returning the toy once she's played with it.

Honor asks if you're coming to parents evening next week?   Also, can we have more pull-ups, please?

(You should see her trying to decide what she thinks of headphones. Keeps trying them on, twisting her head around, then taking them off and just holding them to her ear. She's being very experimental)

Fairly good night disturbed at 5am but settled again with a change and cuddle.

Friday, 18th March

Aggie - Wonderful mood today; lots & lots of singing and cuddles with a very good appetite. I'm sending pull-ups I have for now and will send new pack next week.

Tell us what time you'd like us for parents evening and we'll be there.

Honor here, Ruby had a good am-playing with table-top toys and puzzles, followed by big musical instruments. Drink & crisps for snack-time followed by PE & language work.

Admin today (not my favourite) so Laura covering for me this pm. Could you make 7.15pm next Thursday? Please don't forget staff training Monday so no school until Tuesday.

Good weekend; this good weather meant we could have some nice long walks. Lots of language several new 2-word combinations.

Pretty consistent with "my" "please" and "ta!" She's also using a lot more names and doesn't seem to be referring to herself in the third-person so often

Tuesday, 22nd March

Aggie - Where did that lovely weather go? Although cheery enough Ruby is irritated by all this rain but, as always, thrilled to be going to school. Sending pull-ups as promised.

7.15 on Thursday is fine but I hope you don't mind us bringing Ivan? My parents & sister are at a political rally so no babysitters, I'm afraid. I don't think Ivan would want to be bored with rhetoric whereas he may well be interested in looking at your new computer knowing him!

Honor here, yes, we'd love to meet Ivan on Thursday. Ruby has settled well into work today really enjoyed playing with dough this am. Did PE this pm and seemed to be having a fun time!

Very happy night; Ruby very mellow and cuddly. Down for 10 and slept through with only a couple of changes.

Wednesday, 23rd March

Aggie - Ruby awake for 6.30 and most cheerful. She's been talking a lot and made one-word replies to simple questions. Let's hope this spell of sunny weather is a sign of things to come for Easter.

Leila here, Ruby arrived full of mischief she does LOVE the washing-up liquid!! Did some very nice work with teddy & dolly and her symbols this am. Number work in the pm she's matching numbers beautifully.

Good night; came home with a healthy appetite and in a happy mood. Became even happier as we'd bought her a couple of new outfits for the holiday and she insisted in stripping and trying things on. We had an impromptu fashion parade and Ivan fled the living room in horror Ruby has NO sense of modesty. She was very taken with her new pyjamas, particularly the pair that have a kitten on the front. Down for 11.

Thursday, 24th March

Aggie - Very happy today- stayed in her

pyjamas all night and stayed dry! Adam & I gave her loads of praise and she's all grins and keeps saying, "good girl" and coming for cuddles.

So sorry, I should have warned you about the washing-up liquid obsession. When we are waiting downstairs for the bus unless I watch her the whole time she dashes for the washing-up bottle and pours it all over the sink. I usually compromise by letting her pour a little but then she has to help wash the breakfast dishes. She generally accepts this quite well.

Looking forward to seeing you tonight.

Honor here, Ruby VERY pleased with herself. We've also praised her for being so 'grown up' and she's most smug. Some excellent work today PE & swimming in am and science in pm. See you later tonight.

Thank you for all the information; it was so nice to see all the examples of the work Ruby's been doing with you. Loved all her pictures for Easter she obviously takes after Adam (like Ivan) for artistic ability, my efforts at drawing/painting are quite pathetic. Ivan seems to have been quite excited to have a look around himself but Ruby was way over-the-top. So much so she'd exhausted herself and was very tired in the taxi on the way home. In bed and asleep by 9.30. Lovely!

Friday, 25th March

Aggie - A bit of a grumpy mood today; I decided to risk trimming her fingernails and this led to a blazing row with Ruby screaming her head off. Took a while but we finally calmed her down enough to get dressed. I'm still getting black looks though!

I'm sending in some cards and eggs for everybody. A happy, peaceful Easter to all at the nursery.

Honor here, so nice to see you all, especially meeting Ivan. Thank you very much for all the eggs and cards we're very grateful for all you kindness, 'the girls' send you their thanks too. There are some items from us and a card and present Ruby made in her bag.

Ruby all settled by the time she came in and worked well today. PE & music this am and tap-it box after lunch. She loved the pasta we cooked today and ate loads. Ruby went to the symbol stand by herself before home-time (so no clue by the time of day) and picked out and made the sentence "we go home" without any prompt from us. Hope you have a lovely holiday and we look forward to seeing Ruby on the 11th.

An amazing holiday Ruby loved Easter. Her sleep pattern has been awful, but she has been talking a great deal and using simple sentences. Ruby is also finally wearing clothes inside the house for most of the time, instead of dressing & stripping throughout the day. She comes in from a walk and changes into T-shirt & shorts!

We've also had some definite independence; she suddenly smacked my hand as I was fastening he coat zip and said, "me!" When I held the end of the zip taut she closed it beautifully. She's also making more effort to dress herself rather than waiting for me to do everything for her.

Lots of creative play sticky pictures, drawings and playing imagination-based games. Ruby has also been sharing & playing with Ivan on a semi-regular basis;this is totally new. She's enjoyed singing nursery rhymes both with others and on her own sometimes when she's lying in bed and falling asleep.

I'm aware I'll need to organise swimming for her next holiday as she's complained bitterly about missing out on this. Oh dear, Bad Mommy strikes again!

Monday, 11th April

Aggie - Ruby very excited to be going back to nursery; good appetite and quite amenable to getting washed & dressed. A little anxious waiting for bus. Hope everybody's had a good holiday. Thank you all so much for the cards & Ruby's eggs.

Honor here, lovely to have everybody back. Ruby fine today handed over 2 toys beautifully when told to go for individual work & said "good girl." Unfortunately she ran into a door today and bumped her head didn't cry but had a big cuddle, refused to let us bathe it.

Ruby fine at home; not at all upset about her 'bump'. She settled well and was asleep until nearly 3am when some drunken man rang our door-bell to ask for a cigarette.
After that we were all unable to settle and so had a rotten second-half of the night.

(We didn't murder the drunk but it was tempting...)

Tuesday, 12th April

Aggie - Ruby seems to have shrugged off our disturbance; she's clear-eyed and rested so it must have been enough sleep for her. She ate well and is in a very playful, cuddly mood. No mark left on her forehead and she seems fine now no harm done.

I meant to mention, a new behaviour from the holiday is that Ruby has started 'toileting' and 'feeding' her favourite toys (yes, even the cars). Doesn't do this on a regular basis, just when the mood strikes her. In fact last night I had to stop Ruby from forcing the poor cat onto the potty (Fleur was highly bemused but surprisingly cooperative and seemed disappointed when I stopped Ruby. *sigh*).

Thelma here, sorry, a busy day & no time for proper comment. Ruby reading symbols all the time now!

Much better night to begin with; Ruby used 6 new words appropriately and settled late but into good quality sleep.

Wednesday, 13th April

Aggie - Ruby in an absent mood today; happy & cuddly if you get her attention but otherwise she just drifts into dreamland and stares into space. We think she's just tired as there was another disturbance around 3am (what is that about?) when somebody further up the road started a party with pounding music. I use the term 'music' very loosely.

Honor here, poor all of you Ruby has seemed OK today, not too tired. In fact a good day she <u>loved</u> painting, especially when we gave in and allowed her to get her hands into the mixes. Quite quiet when she did her symbol work didn't say very much- perhaps dreaming as you described.

On & off it's been a terrible night. Ruby full of wind and very upset when using potty. Took a great deal to calm her down- at one point she even bit me and it's been a while since she did that! Did she have sprouts or something similar at lunch? I've literally never known her so explosive, poor child!

After some medicine and soothing we got her to sleep and (thankfully) she got some quality sleep without disturbances.

Thursday, 14th April

Aggie - Whatever caused her tummy upset last night seems to finally be over; Ruby her usual happy self. She's eaten lightly (to be on the safe side) with some milk and juice. I've warned her that she is seeing the doctor today and that I will be coming in to be with her at her appointment.

Leila here, for lunch yesterday Ruby had loads of tinned tomatoes and a little fish-cake. She always eats lots of veg/salad stuff and little of what goes with it.

How did the medical go?

We've found a swimming costume Ruby can use, she had to borrow one today. Seemed fine with the change in her morning routine. We should be going out on the bus tomorrow if we can organise enough help.

Great to know Ruby wasn't disrupted by the doctor and I! The medical was OK; told the doctor about Ruby's skin sensitivity, sleep pattern etc and explained how much she's improved since moving to Upham's nursery. Filled in a form (what a surprise!) that puts Ruby on a register of disabled young people (shouldn't she have been on that already?) Apparently this goes to the Seafront social services & hopefully reminds them of her existence. Who knows, she may even get a social worker!

Anyway, enough moaning. Ruby had a good night; great appetite and nice deep sleep. She hardly stirred all night long.

Friday, 15th April

Aggie - Ruby is in a really, really mischievous mood. She didn't wake up until 8 but she's been on the go ever since. Not bad-tempered but going from one bit of naughtiness to another. However, we've had a lot of big cuddles and she seems calmer.

THANK you so much for use of the costume as it saves me having to drag Ruby around the shops at the weekend when it's busy. I'll take her out on Monday or Tuesday when the shops are quieter and we'll pick what she fancies (Mickey or Minnie maybe?)

By the way, the 'bump' has now turned yellowish and looks horrid but Ruby unaffected. I hope she'll be warm enough in her little dress, I'm sending tights in case. The weatherman promised 17C but who believes them?

Honor here, we managed to organise another 3 helpers so we've had a lovely trip out to the Startleigh garden centre where Ruby loved looking at the fish & small animals. We had a long drive and a picnic in the sunshine. Thank heavens the weather held for us! Hope the weekend goes well.

Good weekend; few upsets but nothing that upset her too much. Excellent appetite and lots of language. In such a happy mood it was even possible to keep her relatively calm when two idiot dog owners allowed their animals to get into a fight outside our house at 12.30 on Saturday. Six months ago it would have meant major hysterics I just sat up with her until 2am giving her cuddles and reassurance and she settled back to sleep. Big improvement!

Monday, 18th April

Aggie - Ruby very happy today; cuddles and lots of talking. She ate a good breakfast but when I gave her a drink of milk she said, "Good girl. Choc'lit" and tapped the drinking chocolate (did not even try to use my hand to do this). I asked her if she wanted drinking chocolate because she had been a good girl today and Ruby replied, "Yes. Good girl. Drink...choc'lit." I was very impressed and gave her the drink; even more impressed when she handed over the cup and said, "More...choc'lit." She was very precise about how she said it and made an effort to look me in the eyes at the same time. Needless to say Ruby got her choc'lit!

Honor here, great news about the chocolate Ruby's making lots of use of appropriate language here too she's been using "more" a lot when she does her symbol work. <u>Full</u> of beans today tried every trick in the book & roared with laughter at her own antics. Lots of symbol reading. By the way, I meant to mention that she behaved excellently on our trip out on Friday- very taken with the fish!

Mixed night; some naughty behaviour but then Ruby was very excited to have Nanny, Grandad and Auntie back home from holiday and with her new swimming costume (more later). When she did settle (11) it was a huge relief!

<u>Tuesday, 19th April</u>

Aggie - Ruby fine today; her usual amiable self. Tremendous appetite today if it stays still long enough she'll eat it (even Fleur is keeping on the move). I did mean to ask you how she'd behaved on the trip it sounds as if they had a good time. I spent yesterday hunting all over to find a Mickey Mouse costume finally located a Minnie one. As soon as I showed her this she shouted, "Mickey!" stripped off and put it on (poor Ivan just covered his eyes and sighed). I couldn't get the wretched thing off her until she fell asleep!

Leila here, glad Ruby likes her costume ('poor Ivan' is right!). Can you send some more knickers in tomorrow Ruby is using the potty for a 'poo' now (yesterday and today) so we'll try her all day in knickers and see if she can manage. Could you please explain to her what is happening? We'll give her lots of praise (and treats) if she's successful.

Good night; she seems very contented. Ate well and had an evening car-ride shortly before bedtime that tired her out nicely.

Wednesday, 20th April

Aggie - Ruby in a lovely, sunny mood but totally uncooperative about washing, lots of biting when doing her teeth (ouch!). I've sent a few pairs of knickers and clothing changes in case of accident. Had a long talk with Ruby about using pull-ups or knickers and offered her a choice she chose knickers and promptly used her potty successfully.

Seems to me she's up for the plan. I've said if she has an accident there's no need to worry as she has plenty of clean clothes and nobody will shout.

I should explain in her previous nursery there was a change of manager. Ruby had been partially dry and usually went without nappies and was changed if wet. Unfortunately the new manager decided that staff wouldn't change children if wet/dirty and after a couple of 'discussions' (ie me being reasonable until she sneered once too often and was told she wasn't fit to run a kennel, let alone a nursery) I put Ruby into nappies for the last two weeks there. I do think it was a mistake and may have held her back about using the potty in your nursery.

We've just been sharing a joke she was eating cereal and finished up so I said, "All done now, Ruby. Put it in the kitchen." Usually she has cereal upstairs and only has a banana downstairs, when she finishes she puts the skin in the bin. Ruby took the bowl and threw it in the bin. I thought she'd been confused until she turned around, pointing at the bin, and said, "Tease" then fell about laughing. My face must have been a picture because every time she looked at me she'd start giggling again. I had to laugh she's got her dad's horrible sense of humour without any doubt.

Honor here, all fine today. Ruby dry until 2.45 and then did a wee in the potty. We've all told her we're very pleased with her, she's a big girl etc etc. If she's happy in the pants we'll leave it like that in school. She's been walking around with the symbol that says "go" today and telling us what it is. Not sure if she's trying to ask to go somewhere?

Thanks for the info about her previous nursery (I understand now why you asked some of the questions you did when looking around here first. I've never heard of a policy like that before and I can understand you being upset). Ruby does seem to enjoy her jokes she's very partial to hiding things and then asking for them with us. She sits and giggles behind her hands as we're looking for them.

Wonderful news! We've made a big fuss of Ruby; telling her what a big girl she is and how proud we are of her. Gave her some cake (bought; my baking isn't anybody's idea of a reward) and Ivan said, "If she goes a whole week dry at school can we have Chinese?" My son:the haggler.

Ruby had an excellent night; late (11.30) but in a lovely, talkative mood and very cuddly.

Thursday, 21st April

Aggie - Ruby very happy today; she ate well and was full of chat. I should mention that we had a car-ride with my sister last night and Ruby got annoyed at her Aunt Becca for tickling her leg. She pointed, frowned fiercely and said, "We go home" as clear as a bell. Was it a threat or a promise?

Honor here, Ruby can't leave the symbols alone at the moment she likes to walk around with them. Beautiful reading of 3 symbols together: "We go school" etc. She really loves to read "We go home," always smiles and looks very happy when reading that one. We're glad to hear she's using her language in different situations and she seems to be improvising and creating new phrases for herself which is a very good sign.

Fine with potty all day used it successfully twice. Tell Ivan it's looking good for his Chinese!

Wow, Ruby loves to surprise us. She's trying to use potty at home now as well. A nice, calm mood tonight ate and slept well. So mellow it's unreal.

Friday, 22nd April

Aggie - Ruby dreamy today; not tired, quite willing to cuddle & play and using language to answer questions but otherwise in a world of her own. It's as if she's seeing and hearing things we can't or is thinking very hard about something. Happy enough but withdrawn.

Thelma here, two staff away today so using back-up helpers. Sorry for short comment Ruby fine, used potty successfully. Have a nice weekend.

Good weekend; we avoided Lord Mayor's day (too many crowds) and had a couple of days at my sister's flat in Cornwall. It's in a little fishing village down on the Lizard and very quiet. Ruby enjoyed herself trolling around the beaches and country lanes despite a little bit of rain. Thoroughly enjoyed visiting shops in nearby village although this led to one funny incident. I took her out on my own and she asked for 'potty' as we were halfway through a field, so I took her into some bushes and said; "Ruby, you can go potty here." She looked at me.

"It's OK, Ruby. You can go here, nobody will mind." The look continued. "Honest, Ruby. It's all right."

Ruby took my hand and said, "Go home. Potty." So we went back to the house and she used her pot and when Adam asked if things were all right Ruby said, "Bad Mommy" so I think I'm back in the doghouse!

Her sleep pattern went completely during the visit but (as I said) she stuck to using the potty. Also ate everything before her I've never seen her so hungry, must be that sea air.

Monday, 25th April

Aggie - Ruby back to her usual routine she made it perfectly clear she does not want to use pull-ups so I'm going with her decision. If you should take her out and Ruby shows a lot of interest in any wild flowers I'm afraid that's down to me. I was getting her interested in touching and smelling all the different types we found on the Lizard (about 25 varieties in all) and she loved that.

Honor here, Ruby in a lovely mood when she came in and fine during the day. We've had two successful wees using the pot and she seems very confident about managing her continence. More tomorrow.

Good night; Ruby tired but very happy. She's obviously enjoyed seeing everybody because we've had a few names used and lots of appropriate language. Down for 10 and 8 solid hours of sleep. Absolute bliss!

Tuesday, 26th April

Aggie - In a great mood today; Ruby ate 2 bowls of cereal and has been full of cuddles and chat. She's been enjoying toy catalogues with me while we wait for the bus.

Honor here, we've had some brilliant reading today Ruby sat with me to read

symbols and read "We go home/ school/ swimming/PE/bus/boat" as well as "We eat cake/crisps/dinner/biscuit." She was very happy and relaxed during this activity.

She has been using the potty as she needs it. We will send the pull-ups home on Friday as we don't think we're going to need them.

You never know where you are with Ruby, do you? Adam and I are thrilled she's doing so well particularly with the potty, as we know she hates being dependent these days more & more Ruby insists on doing things for herself. Seems that reading the symbols is really opening up language for her. Good night very deep sleep.

Wednesday, 27th April

Aggie - Ruby woke up in a lovely, talkative mood and has been very hungry and cuddly. She seems mellow today.

Thelma here, Ruby has had another dry day. Working with dough in the am and made a lovely decoration. Enjoyed

number songs, rhymes and listening to stories in the pm.

Very, very tired and in bed for 8.30pm but we had yet another attempted break-in which had us up for a couple of hours. Ruby managed quite well after extra fuss she settled to sleep well.

Thursday, 28th April

Aggie - Little-miss-sweetness-and-light today despite our broken sleep she's all smiles and raring to go. Lots of fruit with her cereal today.

Honor here, a lovely swimming session this am. First thing Ruby tipped lots of toys out to see what we thought of it puzzled when we made no comment and just helped her tidy up. She thought that over for a while. I have paperwork this afternoon so Laura will cover for me.

Ruby hasn't seemed very 'in' to work today but more inclined to play & explore.

Pretty good night; excellent appetite, lots of cuddles and talking. In bed for about 10pm with good, deep sleep.

Friday, 29th April

Aggie - Ruby in a nice mood; she was surprised to be going to school. Ivan's school has a teacher training day so he wasn't rushing to get washed & dressed to leave with Adam and I think Ruby assumed it was the weekend. Despite the routine change she cooperated beautifully (I think having Dad there to jolly her along helped!) and she was ready as usual.

I've told her that her cousin, Sally, is down for the long weekend and Ruby is all grins Sally doesn't see Ruby often but she always pays her attention and gives her sweets so is very well liked!

Honor here, glad Ruby settled down about coming to school. She was fine here full of mischief. Did a wee and emptied potty across the floor no harm done as it wasn't on carpet just a

mopping job. Hope the long weekend goes well & Ruby enjoys seeing her cousin.

Wednesday, 4th May

Aggie - Ruby a bit grumpy first thing but cheered up after breakfast once she realised she really was going back to school. Eating everything before her. I'm sending a few of her pull-ups for the trip out feel free to use them if you need to. She's usually fine on short trips but for a long walk or car-ride I offer a choice of knickers or pull-ups and Ruby generally chooses pull-ups.

We've been getting a lot of language at the moment & Ruby is answering simple questions/holding very simple conversations. The only continuing problem is she still prefers to turn her eyes away but we're rewarding any eye contact with smiles and praise which does seem to make her more inclined to glance at us.

Leila here, very busy today with trip. Ruby's had a lovely time no problems. More tomorrow.

Well, Ruby obviously enjoyed herself! She came home, ate her tea and then climbed on my lap and chattered away to me (with a lot of eye contact for Ruby) for about 10 minutes. I couldn't really make much sense of what she said but I certainly got the impression she had a good time! Never seen her to animated and chatty.

Great night; really happy and tired.

Thursday, 5th May

Aggie - Lovely mood today; big smile and kiss when she woke. I'm still amazed she managed all that time with no pull-up. Although Ruby does seem to excel in setting her mind to something and then carrying it out if there's any way possible.

Have you noticed lately how much teasing she's doing? Adam and I keep being suckered into searching for things she's already hidden or fetching drinks/snacks/toys she hasn't really lost. She sits there and giggles behind her fingers, eyes dancing with mischief and so infectious you find yourself joining in.

Honor here, yes, she takes great delight in teasing us and watching our reactions. She's a real character. Yesterday went well both at Kid's Day Out & Sports day. Tomorrow is our turn with the bus and we're off to the beach if the weather is suitable please send clothes that you won't mind getting messy and sandy.

Ruby matched numbers 1- 8 today, touched and counted correct numbers from 1-5.

That's great news; we've been sharing counting games & songs with her at home but never had a result like that! Ruby seems to be trying new things everywhere right now. Bit of a grumpy night later (she was a little over-tired) but when she finally went to sleep (12) it was a solid few hours.

Friday, 6th May

Aggie - Nice mood today but full of mischief. As requested Ruby dressed for going out she named some of the clothes while dressing. She seemed very excited to be going out so I hope you all have a good day.

Honor here, no problems today. Very active Ruby into everything. Sorry about her little pumps she was out of them and filling them with stones & sand before we realised what was going on. Hope you can get everything clean she got into a little bit of a mess.

Glad Ruby had such a good time; no worries about mess, that usually goes with her enjoying herself. Good weekend in general one funny but nice incident when Andy was out. I've been feeling a bit run down and after I went downstairs to fetch her a drink I came back upstairs to find this incredible mess Ruby had made and her stood in the middle just waiting for my reaction.

I told her that she had been naughty and started to tidy up but suddenly felt overcome and burst into tears (not like me at all). Ruby seemed to think I was playing at first and then was horrified when she realised I wasn't. She came running over to where I was kneeling, threw her arms around my neck and kept hugging and kissing me saying, "Sorry, sorry." Ruby even made an attempt to pick up some of the mess. For the rest of the weekend she was so well-behaved it was painful!

Monday, 9th May

Aggie - Late start today forgot to set alarm but Ruby very good-humoured about whole thing. Ate a good breakfast and chattered away the whole time.

Honor here, sorry to hear you had such a 'down' moment at the weekend but it's nice to think Ruby responded so sensitively to you and she realised the real effects of her actions. She was furious today when Leila wanted her to do her writing & didn't really calm down until she'd done it with lots of help. We haven't seen that sort of reaction lately she seems a little touchy in general.

Whatever got her so ratty earlier had worn off by the time she came home and Ruby was back to sweetness-and-light all evening with lots of chatting and playing games. Down for about 10 with nice, deep sleep.

Tuesday, 10th May

Aggie - Ruby very pleased with life today; gave me a 5-minute cuddle as soon as she got up and ate a good breakfast with no mess.

Honor here, Ruby a little distracted today but generally did good work. We've been having some discussions about her progress and we wanted to ask your and Adam's reaction to the idea of her moving on from the nursery to infant class in September. I'm admitting about 9 new children in September and we want to make sure that Ruby keeps lots of 1-on-1 attention as that seems to help her most. I am concerned that she might receive less support with so many new children to settle. It's also true that with the progress she's made I don't feel we're really challenging her properly Ruby is comfortably able to cope with what we can offer her rather than trying to master new skills. I believe she would benefit from a more 'class-like' environment where she could work on her studies using the skills she's acquired here with us and with yourselves.

Please think it over and let us know what you think would be best for Ruby her end of year report will be with you shortly and this may help you to decide. I'm on a course tomorrow so Laura will be covering for me.

Ruby in a fairly good mood tonight; ratty now and then but quite prepared to be cheered up again. Rather a late night with a lot of disturbances from the street.

Wednesday, 11th May

Aggie - Ruby out-of-it today; she'll be playing or talking and then suddenly stops and stares off into space. Hope this settles down as it's rather disconcerting it's almost as if she's been dreaming and hasn't quite finished yet and so goes back into the dream.

We'll wait for the report to confirm but Adam & I think Ruby would want to and benefit from moving on in September. She has made a lot of progress and seems to relish facing and overcoming challenges. She's also shown (in however limited a way) some interest in the others in the nursery and we'd be reluctant to see her lose that, Ruby's rarely been able to relate to other children before and it seems unfair for her to lose contact and have to start all over again with completely new people. A few familiar faces might just be what she needs to feel able to cope with changes.

Any idea what happened to her swimming things from Monday? I need to get them washed & dried for tomorrow.

Laura here, Ruby has had a good day with no problems. Quite picky about lunch but did eat a little. We've found her swimming things and washed them for you sorry, they'd slid to the back of the cupboard.

Ruby still quite picky at home; she's been having fruit and milk though so I don't think it will do any harm. We'll keep an eye on it. A quieter night but her sleep was still restless.

Thursday, 12th May

Aggie - Her appetite has picked up slightly but she's in a dreamy mood today and kept losing interest on what she had on her spoon to stare into space. Her eyes don't look heavy so I don't think she's tired from being restless. Hope she's not incubating something.

Honor here, Ruby much more 'with it' by the time she reached nursery. Full of smiles and quite cooperative about doing her work. Swimming pm today and she

was full of mischief splashing other children and staff and laughing about it.

Glad to hear she livened up although she's a cheeky monkey for splashing. I've been caught out at bath-time before now. I blame Adam for encouraging her to splash me because he says the 'Miss wet T-shirt' look suits me. I won't write my reply it's rather rude!

Friday, 13th May

Aggie - Ruby's humour strikes again; I was looking for the book today and suddenly realised she was giggling more than usual. Sure enough when I got her up and checked her seat I found she'd been sitting on it! She's in a lovely mood (if tease-y) and ate a good breakfast.

You may think she looks pale but that's just the sun-block I popped on because the weatherman gave a UV warning for today. I'm really stuck about eye-protection though because Ruby won't use glasses,visors or hats I'm sending in a pair of Mickey Mouse glasses that we've had partial success with as she will consent to wear them if it's very bright.

If you've any suggestions we'd welcome them. Last night we had a 20-minute singing session with "Fat sausages", "Wheels on the Bus" and "Hokey Cokey."   Ruby sang some of the simple refrains to herself afterwards and seemed to enjoy taking turns with us.

Honor here, thanks for all your information. I'm glad you're considering Ruby moving up I think it would help her. Lunch was sausages-and-chips which she seemed to really enjoy.

Trip to shopping centre and the community dentist's van am for check-ups all fine and Ruby seemed to enjoy going up and down in chair. PE in pm with work on catching and throwing skills, Ruby sometimes forgets she's throwing things to people rather than at them.

With regards to her singing she always enjoys that in the nursery and gives us a little song and reads "We go school" on arrival each day.

Enclosed you'll find a permission slip for Ruby to attend Gerry's birthday party on

**Wednesday if you could please complete
and return for Monday I'd be grateful.
Apparently his parents have hired a
bouncy castle, which promises to be a lot
of fun for everyone.**

A very good weekend. Ruby full of mischief but
good-humoured. She's had some sleep
disruption which we put down to the weather
i.e. our neighbours decide to hold parties with
windows open or in their gardens or yards
always about 2 in the morning it seems.

Whole family attended a social evening with
the church on Saturday and Ruby asked for
and successfully used the toilet! Lots of praise
for that one.

Monday, 16th May

Aggie - Ruby's in a very cuddly mood; even
Ivan was given a kiss at breakfast, much to his
disgust! In with her swimming things are a
pair of pants she was sent home in that aren't
hers they're washed and ironed, thanks for the
loan.

Glad the dental check-up went OK, we've
registered her and Ivan with the Pen y Owr

special needs dentist. When we took her along we were worried it might end up a case of 'count the fingers' but she thought it very funny and behaved beautifully. One reason we were concerned is that at her last inoculation our GP stroked her cheek in apology and Ruby latched on so hard I had to hold her nose to make her let go. He's such a sweet man he just said, "Well, I hurt her so she got her own back" and left it at that.

Disturbed night with Ruby unable to settle until about 2am. We're not sure if it was due to nightmares or all the noise in the street.

Tuesday, 17th May

Aggie - Cuddly mood again today and very talkative. She ate a very good breakfast. The party on Wednesday sounds good, Ruby loves bouncy castles in fact she loves them so much you may have trouble getting her off again! Completed permission slip is enclosed.

Honor here, it's been one of those days when she excelled herself lots of lovely symbol reading and several new combinations she'd never seen before &

read them all. Yesterday she tried to read the new labels on the wall display, the only one who did.

Today after register she went around the table touching everybody on the head and trying to count them all something we do every day but Ruby's never attempted before.

This pm Hollybridge Community College swing band came to entertain us Ruby loved the instruments! She really seemed to be 'into' the music, she was bouncing to Glen Miller!

Great night! We all made a big fuss of Ruby & told her what a clever, grown-up girl she is. She walked around all evening with a big grin and in a very nice mood. Very cuddly and slept deeply despite noise around us being dreadful.

I'm not surprised about her liking Glen Miller he's Grandad's favourite too.

Wednesday, 18th May

Aggie - Ruby very happy and talkative today; ate well and into all sorts of mischief, with the naughtiest twinkle in her eye so you can't help laughing.

I have to tell you how thrilled we are with all the progress she's made in the nursery. She seems to change from day-to-day and it's remarkable that she's established such control of her bladder so quickly. I'm sending another pair of knickers and trousers since such an exciting day may cause her problems. I'd wanted to send her in a pretty dress but with this colder weather I've compromised on a pretty top & trousers.

Hope they all have a good time & you and the other staff get a chance to sit down sometime!

Leila here, we're all glad you're so pleased with her we're all proud of how far she's come here with us. A good am and this pm we're here at Gerry's house. <u>Everybody</u> really happy Ruby thrilled with bouncy castle and hasn't come off it yet.

Very late night; Ruby rather over-the-top so we've had to calm her and let her wear herself out.

Thursday, 19th May

Aggie - Ruby a little tired today and rather grumpy at first, cheered up after breakfast. Not at all happy when bus was a little late tough, I say.

Honor here, Ruby rather grumpy here on & off this am things weren't quite the way she wanted them. Fine this pm we made lollies to eat tomorrow.

Ultra grumpy when she got home and in a horrid mood. Stood over her potty and piddled everywhere. When I finished clearing this up I stood up and she head-butted me in the stomach. Definite sign of things to come as we were up with her until 3.30am. She wasn't aggressive again but the least noise or disturbance sent her into screaming hysterics.

Friday, 20th May

Aggie - Back to sweetness-and-light today with no sign of last-night's bad temper at all. Ate very well and made a big fuss of everybody; I think Ruby realised we were all pretty annoyed about last night.

Weather forecast gave a burn factor of 30 minutes today so Ruby sun-blocked. She loves this new sun lotion (it does smell gorgeous) and when I had finished her Ruby insisted on having some to put on her favourite doll. I made sure to keep Fleur out of the way because I'm quite sure she'd have lain there and allowed Ruby to slather her in lotion as well!

Adam & I are still going through Ruby's report (we were a bit busy last night!)but it's bringing it home to us how much more she can do than we've ever expected or realised. She's been playing us and pretending she couldn't do things that she has done in nursery we'll be trying some of those at home so she'll get used to using her skills everywhere, not just where it suits her.

Honor here, glad you were able to look at the report but sorry you had such a bad time with her. I wonder what put her in such a bad mood? We're all delighted with her progress and hope that it continues your persuading her to do things at home as at nursery can only help I believe.

This am we had assembly and PE, followed by singing and language work. After lunch it was tap-it box, some free-play (Ruby chose working on computer with symbols) and then outside to play before eating lollies we made yesterday. Ruby loved her lolly scrunched it all up! Hope you have a good weekend.

Very good weekend; late night on Sunday. I went on pilgrimage to Glastonbury and we weren't home until 10.30pm. It was rather lovely because I'd gone with the children, my parents and sister and a group from the local church, which included a few other children and a lot of elderly people.

Some of the children were rather badly behaved (and some were just bored) but I had a lovely compliment when one dear old soul leant over as we were waiting to leave the bus and said, "My dear, I'd forgotten that well-behaved children like yours existed. They've been treasures." You could have knocked me over with a feather! I'm putting it down to Ivan assisting all the old ladies on-and-off the bus and with moving bags/shopping in his usual helpful way.

Monday, 23rd May

Aggie - Ruby in a huge grump today; she's acting over-tired despite getting a fair amount of sleep. Yesterday obviously wore her out more than I realised! She wasn't eating very well and I offered her some fruit and she threw a wobbler stomping her feet and screaming at me. I told her she was being silly and ignored it all and after a few moments she ran out of steam, sat down and sulked. Hopefully this mood will have cleared for school.

I'm returning a pair of yellow leggings that appeared in her swimming bag they're definitely not Ruby's.

Honor here, Ruby was free of temper once she reached us in fact a lovely smile and nice "hello" to us all. A lovely day all of the children were calm, peaceful and working well this am. I'd invited Hannah, the infant teacher, to visit and meet all the children who may be moving to her class this September. Hannah looked at Ruby's work, heard her reading symbols and went over the details of her individual work programme she's asked me to tell you both to feel free to

arrange a meeting if you want to discuss anything or ask any questions to help you make a decision. All went well and Ruby was at her most charming and made a point of approaching Hannah and examining her very closely, then taking her hand as she walked around the nursery.

On Friday we are going to Waterlands for a class outing.

It sounds as if Hannah has received the Ruby stamp of approval; it's very rare she'll approach somebody strange, taking their hand like that is almost unheard of for Ruby.   It sounds like a good visit and Adam and I will contact Hannah to confirm that we think the move should go ahead.

Good night but restless sleep.

Tuesday, 24th May

Aggie - Late today no problems with Ruby apart from keeping her clothes on!

Leila here, Ruby LOVED bathing the dolls this am. We made fruit salad & Ruby

really enjoyed eating it all strawberries, kiwi fruit, apple, nectarine, melon and banana. Enjoyed every mouthful. After lunch very good counting.

Good night; Ruby very giggly and playful. Using lots of new language.

Wednesday, 25th May

Aggie - Enough time to write in her book today. We're not sure what Ruby going back to stripping is about, it's not that warm. Thankfully she seems to have stopped again. Today she's chatty and cuddly, has eaten well and is presently teasing Fleur with a ribbon.

I'm keeping a wary eye to them because Fleur has no survival instinct whatsoever it seems earlier when we were upstairs Ruby teased Fleur with one of her toys and then threw it over the banister and down the stairs. Sure enough Fleur threw herself right after but fortunately landed safely. Ruby thought it highly amusing and I don't want to find out what mischief she can find in our kitchen to inveigle poor old Fleur into!

(To be fair Fleur is notoriously daft as a brush;

she's dived over that rail on previous occasions). Once when a friend of ours was walking upstairs to the living room she flew over the edge and there was a mutual howl from Phil and her. It took some time to reassure him that I hadn't thrown her at him and Fleur had jumped all by herself.

Although I don't trust the weather not to turn yucky I've sun-blocked Ruby in case.

Leila here, I'm sorry about Ruby's T-shirt she LOVED bubble painting but refused to keep her apron on. I do hope the paint will come out soaking it in cold water first may help. Otherwise today it was language work am and swimming after lunch. Ruby enjoyed bathing the dolls again today she has concentrated for very long periods recently.

(Your poor friend must have been shocked).

Ruby came home happy and had a very good night; lots of sleep.

For the record, from what Adam tells me, it was a toss-up as to who was more traumatised on that occasion; Fleur falling through the air with spread paws and a horrified expression or Philip who suddenly had a maddened, howling banshee land on his head screaming and scratching. Though why precisely he thought I'd throw anything (let alone my cat) at him remains a mystery - a guilty conscience, perhaps?

Thursday, 26th May

Aggie - Slow start today; Ruby VERY reluctant to wake up. It took several attempts before I could get her moving. However, once she was up Ruby was in a nice mood,very talkative and ate a good breakfast.

Honor here, a lovely am. Swimming went well & was enjoyed by all. This pm I have admin work so Laura is covering for me.

We're all looking forward to our day out on Friday.

The weather forecast is good with sun predicted so please make sure Ruby is sun-blocked. We'll leave as soon as everybody arrives at the nursery and stay at Waterlands until 2-2.15pm.

Excellent night; out at a party and Ruby not only asked for what she wanted clearly but joined in some of the children's games briefly. She was singing & dancing until 10.30pm and was asleep as soon as we got home.

Friday, 27th May

Aggie - Really, really mellow today; big smiles and cuddles as soon as she got up. Great appetite, ate everything before her. I've put on sunblock and reminded Ruby she is going out.

****

Dear All,

we've had a great day. All of the children have enjoyed themselves at Waterlands and I think we went on every ride they had! The predicted sun was very strong and I'm so glad everybody remembered to sun-block their child (I wish I'd thought to do the same for myself).

Chicken nuggets or sausages with chips for lunch and ice-cream to follow. We've made sure everybody kept to the shade where possible and had lots of water or juice.

I think you'll find they're all tired tonight. Best wishes for the half-term break from all of us,

Honor, Laura, Thelma and Leila

****

Pretty good holiday; Ruby very playful and talkative. This despite some adverse circumstances grotty weather, assortment of late-night parties, another break-in at the off-licence and Ivan developing a mystery virus. Ruby had a nice little party for her birthday and seemed to enjoy her presents.

****

Monday, 6th June

Aggie - Ruby in a sweet temper today; she's enjoyed her break but seems more than ready to return to school. For tomorrow I'll be sending a chocolate gateaux, crisps, sausage-rolls and sweets for all the nursery is that OK? Ruby wants to bring in her new Noddy video &

I thought she could share that with the others if you don't mind? Please let me know.

Honor here, wonderful to have all the children back and Ruby seems in a particularly happy temper. Yes please, we'd love the video. Glad Ruby enjoyed her birthday and looking forward to a small celebration here at the nursery. The food you've described sounds fine, thank you so much for that.

Ruby used potty perfectly this am and has attempted to use the toilet with mixed success. Could you please sign and return the permission slip for our trip on Wednesday.

To put it mildly a terrific night; Ruby happy & playful. She had a lovely evening with games and singing. Went off about 9.30 very tired but happy.

Tuesday, 7th June

Aggie - Nice mood today; Ruby's a little excited because we've told her that she's having a little party with her friends. Hope everything goes well and there are enough snacks, if there's anything left please use it for everybody's snack-times. I've enclosed Ruby's permission slip for the trip tomorrow (sorry, it was tucked inside her swimming bag).

I should mention we've noticed a lot of jealousy from Ruby to Ivan because of his lunch-box, so much so that we've bought her one of her own. How do you feel about trying her on packed meals? If you've no objection I'll start her on these next week.

The little kilt Ruby's wearing today is only fastened with velcro tabs; I've taken off the outer buckle because she likes to slip out of it and flail it about. I didn't want anybody getting injured if she decides to keep doing this with you.

Thelma here, thanks for everything Ruby loved it all. Ate the lot I'm afraid. Your sausage rolls and cake were VERY popular.

Ever so glad all went well Ruby can so easily tip over into hysterics even when she's been enjoying herself. She was in a brilliant mood until about 9pm when we had a bunch of people decide to sit and drink on our step and then fall into squabbles and fighting. Luckily the police turned up fairly quickly to take away two of the worst although one chap with a head injury was taken into hospital. Can't they do this in their own homes?

Finally calmed Ruby after about an hour and she dropped straight to sleep and was quiet the rest of the night.

Wednesday, 8th June

Aggie - Where did the sun go? Ruby is convinced that if she asks for the sunshine often enough I'll bring it back. I wish I could! Calmer mood today;good appetite and apparently she likes her breakfast. I've been told I'm a "good girl" because I made a chocolate milkshake to finish her meal.

Overnight she seems to have developed a sniffle; I'm hoping this is due to the change in temperature and not a cold as she's not feverish or fretful and her appetite is fine. I've given her a dose of medicine as she's sneezed twice.

Honor here, no sign of cold with Ruby we've had a lovely outing in am. I took Ruby on a trampoline which had her shrieking with laughter. When we stopped she clearly said, "More!" each time. Also took her down a slide with me - a very long bumpy one!

Full of mischief when first arrived at nursery tipping things on to the floor. She settled down after our trip out and we had symbol reading, hand-control and individual work in the pm. I'm on a course tomorrow and Laura will be covering for me.

Bit of a rough ride; a lot of noise kept Ruby disturbed during the night. Had to cuddle & nurse her back to sleep, she went down for around 3.15am. Mom is tired!

Thursday, 9th June

Aggie - Ruby a bit dreamy today (don't blame her, I feel like I'm on automatic pilot) but quite happy. An excellent appetite and most talkative.

Laura here, Ruby happy although tired. We've given her a quiet morning with painting she painted a lovely sea picture with rollers and used several appropriate words spontaneously. PE this afternoon a little tired and difficult to persuade into doing some things.

A good night until 12.15 and the FIRST attempted break-in to the off-licence. No sooner had the police sorted that out and we'd started to settle when there was a second try just before 2am.

We had the same two constables who were very sympathetic and the one who popped in to ask what we'd seen kept Ruby amused by rattling his keys and pulling funny faces. She gave a sneeze and he said, "Bless you" which she loved, it made her giggle to hear somebody other than Mom and Dad say that. Nice guy.

Friday, 10th June

Aggie - I can't believe it but Ruby seems totally unaffected by last night's nonsense; she's happy, lively and full of smiles apart from her sniffle. Very playful and hungry so I don't think her sniffle can be that bad.

Honor here, sorry to hear about your terrible night. All fine with Ruby. She said "circle" and "triangle" when she was doing her shape-work. Enjoyed playing with dough this pm. Hope your weekend is better.

Good night at first; Ruby tired but good-humoured. She's going through another stage of climbing at present and went right up the front of a bookcase in living room and fell off. Luckily I was able to catch her but she did bump her back very slightly on a chair-arm. I must be slowing down because I used to be able to catch her in mid-air when she did this stuff.

Monday, 13th June

Aggie - Ruby in her usual happy mood about being on her way to school; her back has a small, reddened area but she's totally ignoring it, far more focused on eating! Playing shape games before bus came - I had Ruby say "circle" too!

Honor here, you must have had your heart in your mouth to see her climbing like that she does like to frighten us doesn't she? Very cooperative today just did 3 puzzles very nicely. She was cross when I suggested the toilet before swimming she just wanted to go straight into the water. I didn't want that as if her bladder hasn't been emptied she sometimes starts to go as she enters the water. For future I'll obviously have to suggest toilet before even mentioning swimming.

This pm making cakes to enter for the children's show she LOVED cooking.

Finally poor child had an undisturbed night. Happy, playful evening and down for a reasonable hour.

Tuesday, 14th June

Aggie - Ruby really pleased with life today; very cuddly and talkative. Ate a good breakfast and then sat with Fleur on her knee for 10 minutes petting and fussing her Fleur was purring like a motor.

Yes, Ruby does love cooking but best of all she likes eating whatever she's made.

Leila here, busy, busy day today PE and music in am, science in the pm. Ruby exploring all her senses today and with a particular focus on investigating everything using taste, smell and touch. She was concentrating so hard at times that she seemed to lose track of what I was saying to her.

Bit of a naughty evening; couple of incidents of Ruby filling potty and emptying on the floor.

Wednesday, 15th June

Aggie - Ruby had an early start today; very cuddly and enjoyed sharing lots of imaginative games with dolls and teddies feeding, toileting and holding little conversations. She's in such a happy mood!

My mother & sister have read about the Summer Fayre in July and have offered to run a stall as you've appealed for helpers.

Honor here, thank your family so much

for the offer of help, I'll pass that on the organising committee.

Ruby in a strange mood on arrival couldn't find the little Donald Duck she likes to hold. She worked well once she settled down. Went into bigger pool today Ruby loved running in-and-out and splashing.

Ruby a bit grumpy; had a terrible tussle trying to trim her hair. After my second bite I gave it up as a bad job. Late night, up until 2am.

Thursday, 16th June

Aggie - Still grumpy today; ate some of her breakfast and threw the rest around the room. She's been doing a bit of kicking and is generally not-nice to be around today.

Honor here, the grumpiness continued today maybe it's the heat or she's constipated once more. To cheer her up we gave her bubble work this am which she liked. Made a chocolate milk-shake this pm and loved drinking it.

Constipation I'm afraid. Without being graphic Ruby ate very little tea so I gave her some fresh pineapple that tends to have a certain 'loosening' effect. Used potty very comprehensively twice and was back to her cheerful self. Asleep by 9.30 and slept well.

Friday, 17th June

Aggie - A much happier mood today. Ruby kept asking for more pineapple but I thought too much might be bad so refused. She's accepted some other fruit and has enjoyed saying fruit and vegetable names.

Honor here, Ruby much happier this am. Somebody brought in Rosie & Jim dolls & she loved them. She also enjoyed herself bathing the 'babies' said "doll swimming." This pm we had a performance of a small orchestra to listen to Ruby enjoyed their music and seemed to equally enjoy adding her own noises to accompany them. Hope you have a lovely weekend

Better evening; much better appetite and down at a reasonable hour. I'm not surprised she enjoyed the orchestra when she was very little Nanny used to babysit and would be playing orchestral and operatic pieces so I think Ruby may associate them with being fussed over and spoiled.

The weekend has been rather difficult; we're going through another stage of Ruby stripping and refusing to wear her nappies for the night. If we could get her up to use the toilet it might work but she just refuses to wake up and wets everything. I just don't have any way to wash and dry three or four lots of bedding every day. It's quite a problem but we're working to try to get her dry for day AND night the effort will be worth it in the end. I hope!

Monday, 20th June

Aggie - Despite her disrupted sleep Ruby in a lovely mood; very cuddly and talkative. I'm sending money for the Duck Race & trip on Wednesday, it's in a small
purse tucked in her swimming bag.

Honor here, sorry to hear you're having so many bad nights. Ruby fine here today- lots of good individual work and she had fun doing PE today. Thank you

for selling the duck tickets and sending the form for Wednesday.

Are you and Adam happy for me to get Ruby's records up to date ready to send up to the infant class?

Another rough night I'm afraid; she had gone off well by 11.15pm & then somebody decided to let off a load of fireworks (why?). We had seagulls screaming and circling overhead which had Ruby awake and shrieking the house down. This went on until about 2am when it finally stopped and we got her back to sleep.

Tuesday, 21st June

Aggie - Ruby late getting up but in a lovely mood; as I speak she's playing with my typewriter. Touching keys 1-6 and correctly naming them too! She's eaten well and I've sun-blocked her.

We're fine with you preparing her records for infants; Ruby seems excited at the prospect of starting 'official' classes.

Leila here, it's nice to hear that Ruby's using her number skills at home too! She came in happy today had a lovely day. We've had a selection of nice biscuits for three of the mainstreamers last day in the nursery, plus a birthday cake for David this pm. We've noticed that Ruby is more likely to say words if she has a visual image to cue her.

Ruby had a good night which is surprising as there was a really noisy party in one house nearby (and apparently their windows don't shut!) and somebody else let off fireworks around 10pm. Don't know how but she managed to sleep through the lot!

Wednesday, 22nd June

Aggie - In a very good mood today; think she's looking forward to the race. She's eaten well & I've sun-blocked her, the potty has been used very thoroughly. I'd say she's set.

Dear All,

just to say 'thank you' to all of the families for their generous support for the Duck Race, all funds raised will go into the toy fund for the nursery.

We've had a lively day the children enjoyed their walk & picnic but were most excited when we brought out the box containing all of the ducks and the helpers placed them out on the water. Once the race started we followed the ducks down the river to the official 'catching' point and the results were:-

1st Place - Duck 34 Mrs E. Poynter
2nd Place Duck 21 Mr D. Carmichael (congratulations Tracy's Dad!)
3rd Place Duck 19 Mrs I. Harris

All prize tokens have been sent home with the children and, once again, thank you all for your support. We've had a wonderful day out.
Honor, Laura, Thelma & Leila

So glad the day went well. Ruby came home very tired; yawning over her tea and fell asleep as I read her a story. Lovely, deep sleep all night the fresh air must have tired her out.

Thursday, 23rd June

Aggie - Brilliant mood today; happy, talkative and cuddly. She's eaten everything before her and is smiling at everybody. A good night's sleep makes all the difference to her temper.

Honor here, a quiet day for Ruby. She had swimming & language work am with PE & cutting-and-sticking pm. Lots of good concentration and asking very clearly for what she wants.

A 3am night again Ruby tried to settle until there was an accident outside about 11.30 and the two drivers (and their passengers) got into a fight in the middle of the street. Shouting, screaming etc went on until police arrived about 15 minutes later and then it was the better part of an hour before things were sorted out and the damaged vehicles moved away. By then we had no chance to get her back to sleep.

Friday, 24th June

Aggie - Great mood for Ruby today; not upset by her late night and seemingly not tired.

Three yoghurt for breakfast plus fruit. She's very taken with looking through picture books today.

Honor here, Ruby came in happy enough but she did start yawning mid-am. Nice work today language in am and science & individual pm with good concentration. We've noticed her interest in picture books too the images seem to cue her to repeat names of objects or say what is happening. Hope you have a nice QUIET weekend.

Wow, one tired girl! Barely managed to eat her tea before wanting bed. The whole weekend she's been very mellow and relaxed that might be because we seem to have finally reached the end of the student-parties-and-drunken-brawls season. We hope!

Monday, 27th June

Aggie - Ruby very relaxed today; she's eaten well and wanted lots of games whilst waiting for the bus.

Thelma here, we have visits today from some of the children who will be coming

in September and their families, sorry for short comment. Ruby fine today no problems.

Definitely quieter without the students! We had a nice walk tonight and Ruby was tired and ready for sleep by 9. One little accident in night but we soothed her off fairly easily after she was changed and comfortable again.

Tuesday, 28th June

Aggie - One of Ruby's 'dreamy' days today; quite happy but not with-it at all. She's eaten well and played with her toys but isn't talking as much.

Honor here, a good day here. Ruby had obviously brightened up by the time she reached us because we're had some nice, appropriate language today. PE & music am and clay in the pm no problems at all. Tomorrow Ruby & the other children moving get to visit the infant class they'll be going to in September and meeting the staff.

Ruby tired tonight but another disturbance in the street so not down until gone 12. Rested well once we had some peace and quiet.

Wednesday, 29th June

Aggie - Ruby is back to her usual self today. I've told her she's visiting the 'big' class where she's going later this year. She seems very interested and I've been explaining how things will be different but she'll still do things she enjoys and be with lots of people who she knows already. We didn't want her to think that everything would be new as that can be a real trigger for her.

Honor here, Ruby's visit to the infant class went very well. She met all of the staff and had a good look around everywhere. Apparently their selection of toys and tapes was given a very thorough check-over and she seemed pleased by what she saw. Hannah commented that she seemed very relaxed and we're hoping that's a sign she'll make a smooth transition.

What a lovely mood! Ruby came home all smiles and cuddles seems as if she's happy with what she's seen so far. She became a little hyper later on and it ended up a late night (11.30) but she slept well once we got her down.

Thursday, 30th June

Aggie - Very much her happy self today chattering and smiling from the moment her eyes opened. She's up for everything as well; I've been having random bits of mischief and then fits of giggles behind her hands as she watches our reactions. You may get some trouble today if she gets any more hyper.

Leila here, I see what you mean Ruby asked for the toilet today and I helped her but when I bent to fasten her shoe she threw some of her small toys down and flushed them and then screamed with laughter. I'm not sure what exactly went down there but I know that little Mickey & Donald are gone, sorry about that. Ruby thought it all very funny. Aside from that a good day we're putting all of her workbooks and art into a carrier to come home with her. Hope to see you tomorrow. We'll miss Ruby in September.

Oh she's so naughty! I've had similar at home and it's lucky nothing got blocked. Ruby's very full of herself and insisted on looking at her work herself but wouldn't let us hang any up in the bedroom or living room. Late night and slightly restless but no real problems.

Friday, 1st July

Aggie - Ruby happy and excited for her last day at the nursery. We are sending chocolates and presents for everyone as a 'thank you' for all your hard work with Ruby, they're in the large carrier bag. Hope you like them and enjoy your well-deserved rest over the summer. Best wishes to all and our deepest thanks for all you've done for Ruby.

We hope to see you all this afternoon at the Fayre but knowing what a crush these events are it may not happen!

Honor here, thank you very much for the chocolates & your thanks. We've really enjoyed having Ruby in the nursery & will miss her next term. We all wish her every success in the infants. There's a note from Hannah in Ruby's jacket

pocket. Hope you all have a good summer.

I'll miss our chats in the home book. Take care.

****

Dear Parents & Children

I just wanted to offer a big 'hello' to all our new class members and their families. Term starts on Wednesday, 7ᵗʰ September and we are looking forward to sharing a wonderful year of exploration and learning with you all. If you have any questions please feel free to contact me once term commences.

We wish you all a good holiday and look forward to seeing you in September.

Hannah

****

extract from Annual Report for Ruby Redd June 1994

<u>*....SOCIAL AND LIFE SKILLS*</u>

Ruby quickly worked out the routine of the day and this helped her to settle. She likes to know what is happening now and what will happen next. She often refers to the Makaton symbols, e.g. driver, home, to help her structure her day. She can become cross if the routine is altered, but on the whole remains happy and calm.

During the first term Ruby needed to hold a number of small objects, but this has gradually declined to one or two, and she knows when to put them down. She now comes very willingly to do her individual work, and on most occasions will do a group activity, e.g. puzzles, painting, when asked.

During this term Ruby has become dry in the nursery, as well as at home. She previously wore waterproof 'pants' at school, but is now self regulating.

She is able to undress and only needs minimal help with dressing. Ruby recognises all her own possessions and those of other children and she likes to give out the lunch boxes and home books. This is her main point of communication with the others as she tends to play happily by herself. She can find it difficult to share certain favourite activities, e.g. the computer, the weeble. Ruby enjoys all types of musical/noisy toys....

****

Wednesday, 7th September

Aggie - Hi Hannah, Ruby is quite excited about this change but her mood seems very positive. If there are any problems or questions please feel free to contact me at my sister's telephone number as there's no phone in our flat. Hope the day goes well.

Hello, Hannah here, a lovely first day in the infants for Ruby she seems to have settled quite well already. We played with toys, play-dough, painted and sang

rhymes. Nothing too demanding today (or for the next few days).

Just to let you know we normally ask parents to send in 50p per week towards the cost of snacks, drinks and some activities and we ask that you pay this on Mondays. If you need to contact me I am happy to have a chat any time and I can be reached on the school number.

Bye for now, Hannah

Ruby came home with such a smile on her face! She normally finds change difficult to cope with but this new class appears to be fine with her. Quite a relief. An early night as she was tired 9.30 - and solid sleep.

Thursday, 8th September

Aggie - We're so glad things went well yesterday and hope this continues. Ruby's still cheerful despite the monsoon season that has apparently started.

Hannah here, Ruby's had another good day toys, PE, singing (5 Currant Buns song, which she greatly enjoyed) and a

trip to the shops. She was beautifully behaved and seemed entirely happy to take part in everything.

Ruby quite annoyed with us tonight. She came home and wanted to sing the 'Currant Bun' song and we didn't know the words apparently we're horrible parents! She gave us such black looks we had to compromise with a whole range of songs we did know that she finally deigned to accept. Mom & Dad need to try harder!

Friday, 9th September

Aggie - A good night, Ruby was tired last night and slept well. She was grumpy when she first woke but cheered up after breakfast. We've had a lot of language & singing while waiting for the bus.

Ruby had enjoyed herself today she kept 'escaping' into the Senior Unit during playtime (she's very fast, isn't she?) & thought it was great fun! Today she worked on object/picture matching, pencil/crayon work, sensory room. We had a walk around the shops this pm.

Sat in puddle at final playtime so needed a change for her wet bottom we changed her and put the wet clothes in her bag, just to assure you it was not an 'accident'.

Hope you have a lovely weekend.

Patchy weekend Ruby's had a lot of excitement and became rather agitated at times. We think she'll settle down as she gets used to the change of venue & routine.

Monday, 12th September

Aggie - Ruby in a lovely mood today; cheerful and cuddly but she's sneezed a couple of times, hope that's just the change in temperature. Trousers Ruby came home in are washed & ironed and in her bag. Shall I send in a spare set of clothes? I always used to but it's been a long time since she needed a change.

Hannah here, that'd be a good idea, although as I said it wasn't a toilet accident so much as wet grass & water e.g. today Ruby 'escaped' to the senior

unit (off the playground) where they were decorating. She painted the classroom and herself bright yellow before we succeeded in wrestling the brush off her. Ruby thought it all great fun!

My goodness she was yellow! I'm not sure her clothes will ever go back to their original colour but she finally did after a long bath. All her naughtiness seems to have tired her out because she crashed out about 8.30. Of course, that huge storm hit half-an-hour later and we thought she'd be straight up again but she snoozed on we were amazed.

Tuesday, 13th September

Aggie - Ruby bright & happy after her good night's sleep and made a hearty breakfast. I've put a spare set of clothes in her bag.

Hannah here, a better day today no further decorating (so sorry about that!) and Ruby has been taking part more in class today. We're still giving her a chance to settle at her own pace.

Sweetness-and-light tonight but very late settling because of noise from the street sounds as if the students are back! We hope the news we received today will improve our housing situation.

Wednesday, 14th September

Aggie - Just to let you know that we have been offered a new house (after 8 years) and we're in the process of organising a move at present. If Ruby seems rather excited it's probably due to this. She's finally going to have her own bedroom! Which means poor Ivan gets a chance of a decent night's sleep himself. When things are more definite we'll send in details of the address change.

I've already sent in swimming gear in a new bag it's a green towel & a Minnie Mouse swimming costume.

Hannah here, a good day today although Ruby a little distracted. She seems unsure about her new timetable but we're giving her a chance to try everything. Thanks for swimming gear we're sorting out days for swimming later this week.

Congratulations on the offer of a house let's hope it will be somewhere quieter for yourselves and Ruby.

Very moody tonight had a real grump on her at tea-time and we had several instances of screaming and/or shouting. She was late settling (11.30) but fairly settled once she went off.

Thursday, 15th September

Aggie - After her roughish night Ruby unsettled but with a good appetite. Very uncooperative about getting washed & dressed (bit of a bite I'm afraid) but brightened up once ready and happy to wait for bus.

Hannah here, Ruby a little irritable first thing but cooperated nicely for PE. She became very giggly this afternoon and seemed to enjoy playing with musical instruments and drawing 'faces'.

Stayed in her giggly mood all night she even fell asleep chuckling to herself. Ivan commented he thinks she's planning something, knowing Ruby he could be right!

Friday, 16th September

Aggie - Ruby's still pleased with herself lots of smiles and a few cuddles as well. She does she very puzzled by all the boxes and mess of packing so I'm hoping that isn't going to upset her.

Hannah here, I'm not sure if the two things are connected but a 'huge' puddle on the classroom floor at lunchtime (Ruby took off her clothes announcing they were 'wet'). Where did all that liquid come from in such a little girl? We cleaned and changed her and didn't make a fuss.

Today she had 1-to-1 work, sensory room, singing and games in am. A long walk in the pm. Have a lovely weekend.

Rough weekend; lots of disrupted sleep and patchy appetite. We've also had huge amounts of mischief!

However, once we make our house move (hopefully next Friday) we're keeping our fingers crossed things (and Ruby) will settle down.

Monday, 19th September

Aggie - Ruby singing and dancing today- is that something she's picked up in class? I've never had that much success in dancing; she tends to look at me as if I'm crazy or covers her eyes if I dance on my own and trying to dance with her leads to sitting on the floor and drumming her heels.

Hannah here, Ruby has been as busy as ever in school but happy into everything but nothing unusual & not distressed when removed from play to do something else.

Cutting & painting apples for Harvest display. We had a practice of singing Harvest songs which Ruby livened up by almost managing to take her clothes off. Afterwards she was very interested in a story about Floppy the dog. Worked on doll play and jigsaws.

Much, much better night; Ruby happy and cuddly. Went to sleep at a reasonable time (10.30) and slept through.

Tuesday, 20th September

Aggie - Ruby in a lovely mood today; she's eaten well and played a few games.

Taking off her clothes has always been a problem with her but we did hope it had disappeared for good this time. Perhaps all the disruption of the move is making her tense and bringing this on - so we hope that in the new house we can persuade her to save stripping off for her bedroom and keeps her clothes on everywhere else. Unfortunately she thinks it's really funny.

Hannah here, she kept her clothes on today at least! Lots of singing today 5 Currant Buns, 5 Little Frogs etc. Work on hand coordination, making clay 'apples' and painting tree trunks for our apple orchard. Hydro tomorrow.

A good night Ruby in a lovely mood and settled to bed early (9.30), slightly restless but not at all unhappy.

Wednesday, 21st September

Aggie - Ruby a bit grumpy when she first woke

up but got washed and dressed and brightened up after breakfast.

Hannah here, Ruby lovely today. Coloured autumn leaves and looked at photos this am. Hydro & singing this pm.

Another good night (I could get used to this!) and very good, relaxed sleep.

Thursday, 22nd September

Aggie -Ruby very cuddly this morning I've been telling her all about her new bedroom and she seems excited. Just a little more work and we're ready for the move tomorrow.

Hannah here, PE this morning, music & play-dough and went shopping in pm for 'apple' foods. It's minibus day on Monday I think we'll go to Tamarstock Park. Will write more tomorrow.

Really busy tonight and Ruby very unsettled late settling but did finally sleep well.

Friday, 23rd September

Aggie - Ruby fine today as soon as she's gone

we're moving the last of the furniture and she'll come home to the new house tonight. Half-excited and half-dreading her reaction.

Hannah here, Ruby had a wonderful day today, we've made a great fuss of her. Good luck in your new home and have a good weekend.

Monday, 26th September

Aggie - A wonderful weekend! Ruby thrilled with her new house (especially having her own bedroom). She has been very happy and shown little sign of disruption.

Hope she enjoys her day out.

Hannah here, so glad to hear move went OK. Ruby seems as happy as ever in school. She managed to eat lots of paint today but her stomach doesn't seem upset. Enjoyed her trip out.

Hydro tomorrow.

She's such a tired girl tonight. I think all the excitement and then a day out wore her out.

In bed and asleep by 8.30. No sign of problem from the paint she does have a taste for eating the strangest things and I have to be so careful with her and cleaning products.

Tuesday, 27th September

Aggie - Another disturbed night; Ruby had a wet bed but we got her changed and settled quickly. Otherwise she's in a happy, playful mood. Lots of games this morning not very interested in breakfast but did have 2 yoghurts.

Hannah here, she's been happy here too! Thoroughly enjoyed hydro.

Restless night. We're not sure if it's a reaction to all the change or not. It's very quiet here compared to our old flat -you'd never think we're almost in the city centre. Apart from the cathedral bells for mass it's generally peaceful and we even have early birdsong, although that stops when the builders arrive to work on the unfinished flats nearby!

Wednesday, 28th September

Aggie - No ill effects from her disturbed night;

she seems very happy now. She ate well at breakfast and is very bouncy.

Hannah here, Ruby has been great again today she's been playing with water & the new sand in the playground sand-pit. Aside from that had music today, language work and a walk to round off her short week. Hope you have a good time over the long weekend.

Monday, 3rd October

Aggie - We had a nice break in general; a few wet beds but we're sure it's just the disruption of the move. She's very happy and playful with lots of talking, she's also been answering simple questions for us recently. A lot more responsive in all.

Hannah here, today we went for a walk instead of hydro. It was too good an opportunity to miss as this lovely sunshine was a delightful surprise so late in the year.

Lovely evening and Ruby's been amusing us all with her singing and more of her funny little dances she seems to enjoy the attention. Down for 10.30 and slept well.

Tuesday, 4th October

Aggie - Ruby in a nice mood today we're putting it down to the improvement in her sleep pattern. Surprisingly patient waiting for bus.

Hannah here, parents evening is on Thursday, 13th can you and Adam make a 7.15pm appointment. Ruby quite focused on her work today enjoyed singing, PE and music today with a short walk around the shops.

Played in the garden with Ruby tonight, she's very taken with it as this is something we haven't had before. Adam and I are making plans for how we can organise things to be able to grow fruit/vegetables and have play-space for Ruby & Ivan. Good sleep tonight.

Wednesday, 5th October

Aggie - Disturbed night but Ruby still bright and cheerful. She has a truly amazing appetite today I've never seen so much food disappear so quickly. Adam and I can make the 13th appointment, although we may have to bring Ivan as well if my family can't babysit.

Hannah here, a lovely singing session with her this morning some good anticipation. Hydro tomorrow.

Ruby in fits of giggles tonight as we saw a squirrel running about on some of the builders gear and the site cabin. Cheeky little thing was searching for food from the look of it. She loved the sound of the word squirrel and kept repeating it over and over, although the pronunciation was very difficult for her. A late night but good, solid sleep

Thursday, 6th October

Aggie - Ruby very reluctant to get up today she really likes her new comfy bed and snuggling up with her teddy bear.

Hannah here, it was all about hedgehogs this am made large leaf hedgehog & clay hedgehogs. Sensory room and singing in pm.

Horrible children from further down road were around in the building area last night trying to vandalise the statues in the garden of the old people's flats. When they were chased off they tried throwing rubbish into garden until we went and threw it back. Ruby a bit disturbed by all the noise but managed to settle to sleep.

Friday, 7th October

Aggie - A happy mood today and Ruby's chattering a great deal she really likes the words 'hedgehog' and 'squirrel'. We always call her a little hedgehog (hotchi witchi from Adam's Romany roots) because when she's falling asleep or waking up she wrinkles her nose and makes a cute little snuffling noise just like the hedgehogs you hear running about in your garden sometimes.

Hannah here, into everything today but very happy. Singing, colour matching work, cutting & painting for Harvest picture. Sorry to hear about problems with neighbour's children.

I called Ruby's picture of a hedgehog "Hotchi Witchi" today and she smiled and

touched her own chest she seemed to know what it meant but likes it as a name.

Good weekend with Ruby lots of fun in garden and a much better sleep pattern. The brats were about again but seem to have learned to leave us alone now.

Monday, 10th October

Aggie - Ruby cheerful and cuddly today she's very focused on checking for the bus right now.

Hannah here, today Ruby worked on turn-taking, object/picture identification, modelling and making marks on paper in am. Hydro in pm hence wet hair! Sorry.

I'm out until Thursday so Gail will write comments.

Not much appetite for tea but perked up after a drive and had a big supper. Ruby settled for 10 and slept well.

Tuesday, 11th October

Aggie - Ruby a bit puzzled when I said no Hannah today but I explained that Gail would be with her instead she gave me several funny looks, then seemed to accept what I'd said.

Gail here, Ruby did some turn-taking work today and this afternoon we went for a walk. She's been fine no problems at all.

Nice to have Ruby take the change so well; she's coped so well with lots of changes recently. Early to sleep and slept through.

Wednesday, 12th October

Aggie- Ruby has eaten well and is reasonably calm. I did get bitten twice when cleaning her teeth which is pretty uncommon these days.

Gail here, Ruby has been fine today quite her usual self. Individual work this morning with singing and painting this afternoon.

Good night again. Not undisturbed sleep but

she did settle and managed to sleep through some noise at the back of the house.

Thursday, 13th October

Aggie - A lovely mood today; told her Hannah is back and got another series of funny looks. I'm not sure Ruby believes me sometimes which is rather unfair, it's not like I'm in the habit of fibbing to her!

Hannah here, another happy day Ruby seemed pleased to see me again. Today she worked on singing, colour sorting &matching, sensory room and painting. (You'll be pleased to hear that now I'm back that's the last course I have for a while so less disruption for Ruby & the others).

Nice to see you and have a good discussion about the progress Ruby's making so far. We did think that the taxi ride would help Ruby to have another good night but I suppose all good things come to an end. Ruby's sleep pattern disappeared tonight she just went on and on. Finally got her to sleep at 3am. Mom & Dad collapsed!

Friday, 14th October

Aggie - Today she's in a sunny mood. How does that work exactly? We're both re-enacting Night of the Living Dead and she's bouncing around with a cheeky grin and lots of singing. I don't know how she does it.

Hannah here, Ruby absolutely fine today. Her latest toys are the doll, a bath and about 1 inch of bubbly water (although she does like to add some plastic frogs for variety sometimes!). Hope you have a good weekend and get some better sleep with her.

We've spent the weekend trying to wear her out with lots of outings and games it's had some success so she's sleeping a little better again.

Monday, 17th October

Aggie - We're not quite sure but Ruby's general behaviour and lack of appetite suggest to us that she may be developing a cold. She's no temperature or sneezing but she pretty well only loses her appetite like this when there's some kind of sleep problem.

If there's any change in her condition or you have concerns don't hesitate to get in touch and we'll bring her home. I'd really prefer not to send her in today but she's upset at the idea and I've got no real symptoms to point to it's just a nagging feeling that there's something wrong.

Tuesday, 25th October

Aggie - Well, it was all very dramatic having to pick her up like that and it's been a rough few days for the poor child. However, the doctor now gives her a clean bill of health so I'm sending her back today. She was grumpy when I woke her but became all smiles when she saw 'school' clothes coming out of the drawer.

I hope she'll still be able to take part in the Harvest festival despite her missed rehearsals with her tummy bug I'm sending in a pumpkin for her to decorate.

Hannah here, so lovely to have Ruby back again. She has been fine today so OK we let her go into hydro this pm. We've dried her hair with a hair-dryer so she

should be fine. Hope she's all right tonight of course she'll be taking part in the next rehearsal tomorrow.

Glad things went well. Ruby very tired tonight but fought to keep going until 11pm. She seems to have loved being back in class and seeing everybody I think being ill for so long made her think school had gone away forever.

Wednesday, 26th October

Aggie - No surprise today that Ruby didn't want to get up. A large bowl of cereal and banana cheered her up but she remains rather dreamy but happy and calm.

Hannah here, Harvest festival rehearsal this pm Ruby 'sat' very well. Thank you for the pumpkin, by the way, it looks lovely and juicy.

Ruby tired tonight and was down for 8.30 but woken around 1am by street noise (fire engine with lights flashing) from an emergency. Finally settled her again after 2am.

Thursday, 27th October

Aggie - A bit tired today but pretty cheerful and she seems excited about the coming day.

Hannah here, Ruby was lovely in Harvest today. A bit naughty later in the am all part of her routine stuff! We survived and so did Ruby (despite her best efforts).

Sounds like our Ruby, all right. A good night.

Friday, 28th October

Aggie - Bright as a button today and raring to go. I don't know where she gets her energy from but I wish she'd spare some for us!

Hannah here, Ruby's had a wonderful day lots of finishing pictures and other projects before the holiday. Hope you have a relaxing time with her. Term commences Tuesday, 8th November.

Lively holiday; Ruby up to all sorts of mischief. She's been using lots of appropriate language and kept a reasonable sleep pattern. As her appetite's recovered she's developed a new passion for fish dishes particularly trout.

Halloween was great fun; Ruby loved our little party and had a good time eating gruesome treats, making wolf howls (Adam's influence I'm afraid) and 'ghost' noises.

Tuesday, 8th November

Aggie - After her good night's sleep Ruby was awake bright and early in a really nice mood; she's ready to get back to school I'd say. I'm sending in money for firework display although I do worry we may not be able to attend if Ruby becomes upset.

Hannah here, Ruby very happy and full of mischief. We've kept her clothes on (the colder weather's a blessing as being cooler obviously makes naked seem less attractive!) but she's grabbed every chance for a bit of fun. It's lovely to see her bounce back so well from that horrible bug (she looked SO pale and miserable when you had to pick her up it worried us). Ruby's got that naughty twinkle back in her eye.

Tell me about the stripping! There's a reason we sometimes call her Rudie Redd, Fastest Striptease in the West! She can be out those clothes in nothing flat & manages to hide them so you're scrabbling to keep her covered up. Modest she ain't!

Anyway, glad to hear she's had a good day (even if you haven't, sorry) and she's had relaxed evening and settled for about 11pm.

Wednesday, 9th November

Aggie - Ruby has a gleam in her eye today. We've been on tenterhooks waiting for her to do something but nothing so far lots of giggling behind her hands. Hope she doesn't do anything too horrible.

Hannah here, Ruby is very giggly but she's not been particularly naughty or mischievous just very amused about something. She's had a wonderful time cutting-and-sticking a collage picture for our firework display. I'm sending your tickets in her bag.

After Ruby had gone I found what had her so amused. I wasn't. Suffice to say tonight we've been going over "This is your bed. This is the toilet. You don't sleep on the toilet and you don't sh** in your bed because Mommy really doesn't need her stomach turned before breakfast. Ugh!!

When we'd had that discussion I think Ruby realised she'd blotted her copybook with me so she vied for Adam's attention and gave me black looks most of the night. Too bad. Thank you for sorting out our tickets.

Thursday, 10th November

Aggie - It seems that Ruby has decided to forget about yesterday; I got a lovely smile and chatting as soon as she woke with no sign of temper. We've let the matter drop and hope for no repeats. Let us know how things go today.

Hannah here, what a naughty girl! It does explain all the giggling we were checking to see if she'd done something we'd missed and she obviously had, just

not here. No sign of any 'messy' behaviour here today she's done singing, music and PE am with hydro pm. I really wish you the best for tonight that there's no repeat of her soiling.

No soiling, a bit of tantrums because of odd fireworks being let off and seagulls screaming about overhead. She dropped off around 11pm and only needed changing once.

Friday, 11th November

Aggie - Awake bright and early with a good appetite and so sign of upset from last night let's hope that lasts through the firework display tonight. Look forward to seeing you then.

Gail here, Hannah in emergency meeting for another child first thing so I'm covering. Ruby did some turn-taking work in the am she doesn't like having to wait her turn but will accept it with some help. A nice long walk in the pm they've been enjoying the local scenery. Have a good weekend.

Well, Friday fireworks at Upham went better than we hoped Ruby does like the pretty colours even if the bangs aren't so popular. Other than that a ghastly weekend her sleep pattern disappeared between fireworks, seagulls and dogs.

Monday, 14th November

Aggie - Ruby has eaten well today and is reasonably calm now. Biting a bit today when I cleaned her teeth had to hold her nose to make her let go. Hopefully she's saving that sort of thing just for me.

Hannah here, sorry to miss you on Friday (as Gail said an emergency came up and we had to pull a late night working things out). Ruby has been fine today her usual self. She's done individual work this am with singing & painting this afternoon.

A lot better tonight; enjoyed her tea and spent the evening playing games and singing songs with us. When somebody let off a late firework that set a dog barking she commented, "Bad dog. Shut up!" which I thought was a pretty calm reaction for something that frightens her so much.

Tuesday, 15th November

Aggie - Ruby nice and rested today and looking forward to hydro. That said I can't find her swimming costume anywhere I've put in her old one but it's pretty shabby.

Hannah here, another happy day for Ruby. Today she worked on singing, colour sorting/matching, sensory room and potato printing. No hydro today as a problem with the heating. We've checked for the costume but no sign.

Rather a rough night; Ruby's sleep pattern has gone again.

Wednesday, 16th November

Aggie - Ruby better-tempered today; she was deliberately opening her mouth whilst eating today to show us her food I told her she looked like a cement mixer and she sputtered and laughed so much I ended up wearing her breakfast. Do you want me to attend Ruby's vaccination tomorrow? I've always come along before but I gather most parents stop coming after nursery and I don't want to make her feel like a baby.

However we did have that incident of her biting our GP a few   years ago and I don't want anybody getting hurt. Being a 'big girl' is important to Ruby and the last thing we want is to compromise that, but we also don't want her thinking it's OK to hurt people because she's upset.

Hannah here, if you think Ruby will be OK tomorrow we'll look after her with pleasure. Any problems and we'll call you straight away. We've assessed the risks and I'll take her in myself just in case she does get snappish. The swimming costume turned up in her PE bag for some reason it had been washed and dried, just put back in the wrong place.

Lots of clay-modelling today (we had a bit of a struggle to stop her eating the clay) and she obviously enjoyed 'squishing' clay through her fingers. We managed to keep most of it out of her hair (sorry). We are giving a school assembly on the 25th November lots of work to do preparing

'Most of it' was right when she came in the door I had to carefully keep my face straight and Adam and Ivan arrived and had giggle fits at the sight of her (which Ruby did NOT approve of!). A nice bath with LOTS of shampoo fixed her up and she went back to smiles again. Pretty poor quality sleep tonight no particular reason we can see.

Thursday, 17th November

Aggie - I've explained that Ruby will be having an injection today and that she will be going with one of you and not Mom because she's a big girl now. She seemed totally relaxed about the whole thing I, of course, am a gibbering wreck but that's my problem not Ruby's. Hope all goes well and don't hesitate to call me if I'm needed.

Hannah here, no problems today. Ruby accepted my holding her hand as she had her vaccination and even watched the needle go in. She wasn't best pleased about it but soon cheered up when offered a lollipop (sugar-free!) by the nurse. Some nice work on numbers and turn-taking today.

Thank you so much for taking care of her today. I do appreciate you taking such a risk for her as Ruby doesn't let go easily once her teeth latch on (I've got the scars to prove it) and we're lucky she's never really tried to snap at anybody other than myself (and our GP) but there's always a first time. Ruby was quite unmoved about the whole thing but did like being told what a 'big girl' she'd been. We had ice-cream to celebrate getting that out of the way.

Friday, 18th November

Aggie - Very mellow today; big smile and hello as she woke today. She seems happy and looking forward to school.

Hannah here, lovely day with Ruby today she seems to have forgiven me for taking her for the injection! Today she worked on matching objects/pictures and singing am and cutting-and-sticking this pm. Hope it's a good weekend.

Not a perfect weekend but we've had much worse. Ruby's been patchy with sleep and rather 'messy' but we're working on that.

She's been singing some new little song to herself no clear words but she's making sounds that you can **almost** understand. I assume that is for the assembly.

Monday, 21st November

Aggie - Funny mood today; she started out rather cross for no particular reason and then starting giggling (again for no reason I could find) and has stayed that way since.

Hannah here, very good hydro session today Ruby really enjoying doing her stretching exercises. She's been using lots of words recently and today she counted some 'spots' up to 5 great work.

I found out what the giggles were about apparently Ruby didn't like her new cereal because she must have 'lost' it while I was in the kitchen fetching her some milk. She 'lost' it all over Fleur who didn't seem to particularly mind she was licking off milk and munching odd bits of cereal from her fur for most of the morning.

Ruby relaxed tonight and grinning whenever she saw Fleur. Down for 9.30 and slept well.

Tuesday, 22nd November

Aggie - Happy Ruby today and I've shut Fleur upstairs to avoid a repeat of yesterday. She's calmer and (I hope) less up for mischief.

Hannah here, a fine day today. Ruby still using lots of words: "swing", "book", "Thomas"(Thomas the Tank engine) and phrases, "I can't" (she likes that one!), and "sorry." It's a lovely selection and she seems to be using them appropriately.

Ruby lively tonight; kept going until 1am and then crashed, we were VERY thankful.

Wednesday, 23rd November

Aggie - Slow start today but she's happy enough. Ruby seems off her cereal again but she's settled for fruit and yoghurt.

Hannah here, Ruby using lots of words today - "school", "bag", "can't" and"cat" among them. She's been doing some painting today although we had to stop her because she started trying to drink

**the water the brushes are washed in.
She insisted it was "tea."**

I have the same problem with her bath-water;
she insists it's "soup" (which she adores) and
keeps trying to drink it. Good night tonight;
down for 9pm and slept well.

Thursday, 24th November

Aggie - Clear rejection of cereal today so I
made porridge unfortunately this meant that
Ruby had to dash for the loo about two
minutes before the bus came. Must
remember for future to only serve at
weekends! Bad Mommy strikes again.

**Hannah here, Ruby had to make a dash
for the toilet once she arrived here but
fortunately seems to have settled. She's
been working with photographs today
looked at photographs of 5 peers and 3
staff members and handed them to the
correct people, making very good
attempts to remember and pronounce
names correctly. She's been very good
today.**

It's our assembly tomorrow and we've been practising 'birthdays' as our theme so could you please send Ruby in a party outfit (we'll do our best to keep it clean I promise). She'll also be dressed as a 'shop-keeper' part of the time but we have a few items that will go over most dresses.

We've had a fun evening letting Ruby try on different outfits and choose which she wanted I put my foot down about her wearing the white dress but otherwise left it to her. She's picked her favourite pink which is good as it's easy to sponge off if she spills so no problems. Down for 10.30 and nice sleep.

Friday, 25th November

Aggie - Ruby most excited at thought of assembly. We had an impromptu performance of "Happy Birthday" sung to Fleur and demands for "cake." Hope all goes well today.

Gail here, Hannah has had to take time for personal reasons today so I've covered for her today. Children had a wonderful assembly and Ruby looked lovely in her pretty dress and sang

beautifully. Teacher training on Monday so week commences on Tuesday, 29th November. Hope you have a good holiday.

Took Ruby to see the Christmas lights turned on over holiday she had the fireworks (why do we have fireworks with everything?) but loved the lights. She said, "Daddy Chris's" when Santa appeared and was much happier when the noise had died down a little.

It's been a busy 'holiday' and between trying to prepare Ivan for a spelling test (he does stress about spelling, poor kid) for the first day back at school and keep Ruby from doing horrible things to Fleur (which Fleur seems to quite enjoy *sigh*) Adam and I are ready for a break of our own!

Tuesday, 29th November

Aggie - I'm glad the assembly went so well and that Ruby behaved, her dress came through remarkably well considering. Sorry to hear about Hannah's problems and hope it's nothing too serious?

Gail here, Hannah is back on Thursday

her father passed away suddenly. I've spoken to her and assured her that the class is fine and we can cope until she's able to come back to us.

Ruby's had a lovely day today full of fun but no nastiness at all. She's been teasing and grinning at us with the wickedest smirk imaginable on her face. Some good number matching today.

So sorry to hear about Hannah's loss, I can't imagine how she feels. The last thing she should be worrying about is the class I'm sure they're fine even if they do miss seeing her. Ruby had a late night but asleep by 11.30 although restless.

Wednesday, 30th November

Aggie - We've got the teasing thing going today; she's been putting things like her shoes out of sight and then pretending to look for them when we ask where they've gone. She had Adam convinced her bag had been left on the bus or something until I pointed out she'd stuffed it behind the couch before he came downstairs. Ruby frowned at me for spoiling her joke!

Gail here, Ruby still cheeky when she reached nursery. Asked for toilet and then took opportunity of new helper, Tanya's, distraction to throw a bunch of little toys down and flush. We'll have to have the plumber in as something must have stuck because it keeps flooding when we flush. We're using the main toilets for now.

Aside from this she had hydro in am and painting & sticking in pm

I'm so sorry! Ruby really is bad about the toy thing we've had it at home but not in a while. I've told her off and said she has to leave the little toys behind in future if she's going to do things like that. Poor sleep tonight, not really settling.

Thursday, 1st December

Aggie - Hannah, both Adam and I send our deepest sympathies to you and your family. If there's anything we can do to help please feel free to ask we've both lost close family and know how things can pile up inside.

Ruby has missed you and we both got a big smile when we told her you were coming back today. We've been getting a lot of counting, looking at books and making random spontaneous comments recently and you may see some examples of this yourself.

Hannah, thank you for your kind comments. It's been a very difficult time but I've been looking forward to getting back to the class particularly as we have the Christmas service to prepare for. Ruby insisted in sitting on my lap and put her head on my shoulder when I was reading a story today.

She certainly did miss you didn't she? Not often Ruby does that for anybody. I hope you find things will get easier now you're back in your routine. If anything about the infant class (and Ruby) can be said to be routine that is!

Friday, 2nd December

Aggie - Awake early and lively as a cricket; Ruby's all excited and we're not sure if it's about the nursery or because we've been getting out the decorations to check if they're still suitable for another year.

Hannah here, Ruby is very excited. Yesterday we were looking at ideas for our contribution to the Christmas service and we were thinking of dressing in national costumes. Ruby enjoyed looking at all the different outfits and we wondered if you have any ideas for something she could wear?

Nice singing today we're taking part in several carols which she seems to love. Hope you have a good weekend.

All that singing tired Ruby out; she came home yawning, barely made it through her tea and her eyes were button-holing as I walked her upstairs to her room. She fell asleep still singing very faintly to herself I think it was Jingle Bells but it can be hard to tell if she chews her teddy at the same time.

Monday, 5th December

Aggie - You know on children's shows when the presenter suddenly pulls out a completed project and says, "Here's one I prepared earlier",and looks smug. That's me right now.

I've got a lovely little Polish costume that is almost perfect for Ruby she'll have to use a flowered T-shirt because the embroidered blouse is rather large but everything else fits just fine. Take a look and tell me if it's suitable.

Hannah here, thank you for the costume she'll look lovely. Lots of excitement this pm as the Christmas tree was put up & Ruby was desperate to hang <u>all</u> the baubles.

Yes, we put up our tree at the weekend and she loved taking part in that. Although we noticed she was pinching the chocolate decorations when we weren't (she thought) looking. I mugged and pretended amazement, "The chocolate decorations are gone. Who's taken the chocolate decorations?" "Ivan," Ruby clearly replied and grinned. He REALLY wasn't impressed - second year she's tried to blame him!

Good sleep tonight.

Tuesday, 6th December

Aggie - TWO bowls of cereal today; somebody's found her appetite again.

Hannah here, we've had a lovely day making Christmas decorations today Ruby has managed to get glue and paint everywhere (I don't know how we watched her and she still managed to do it).

She's greased lightning when she wants, our Ruby. You weren't joking about everywhere I even found glue and sequins inside her knickers when I was changing her for her bath. Either she wanted to decorate inside her clothes as well as the outside or she's got a future as a smuggler.

Wednesday, 7th December

Aggie - Happy little girl today; Ruby was singing and dancing before I was even into her room. Good appetite today and she's finally stopped dropping stuff down to Fleur (who begs like a dog it's so embarrassing!).

Hannah here, Ruby looks great in her costume so pretty. She was very good in church for the first rehearsal.

Ruby obviously enjoyed the rehearsal, she came home and gave us a performance all by herself. We've had a nice evening with songs and games and she settled for 10pm, slept well.

Thursday, 8th December

Aggie - In a bright and happy mood today; she ate a good breakfast and Ruby seems ready for her next rehearsal. Hope things go as well today.

Hannah here, Ruby looked lovely this morning even though she would not wear her beads, belt or head-dress! Very well behaved and worked hard to complete a large picture of Father Christmas this pm. The service is tomorrow.

Ruby does like her own way, doesn't she? She's been very happy tonight but reluctant to settle down for about 11pm and then slept well.

Friday, 9ᵗʰ December

Aggie - I'm crossing my fingers for the performance she's in a lovely mood and I think Ruby will cooperate today.

Hannah here, Ruby was beautifully behaved both on-and-off stage she even consented to wear the full costume which looked lovely. We've taped the performance for parents to watch. I'll be organising a rota for parents to be able to borrow and watch this. Have a good weekend.

I was in Birmingham with my sister visiting my niece for the weekend but Adam tells me Ruby has been using lots of new words and sang "Fly Away, Peter, Fly Away,Paul" using two little toys. She's certainly in a relaxed and friendly mood I didn't even get frowned at for being away!

Monday, 12ᵗʰ December

Aggie - Ruby in a really hyper mood today; not sure what the problem is but she's really up for any type of mischief. I've had drinks and food everywhere today so I suspect you're going to have some trouble.

Hannah here, Ruby has driven us 'mad' today she keeps picking up small toys, rushing to the toilet and putting them down then flushing. Thought it was very funny. This pm I found a <u>red</u> chair which I have been sitting her on while gently hold her wrists on her lap and look very sternly into her face. This seemed to work a lot better and she stopped giggling. I told her we can't afford to lose toys at the rate she gets through them!

I'm not really cross (it's just Ruby being Ruby) but I think she needs to start understanding that what she does has consequences ie keep throwing your little toys down the toilet and we run out of toys for the classroom.

Sounds as if Ruby has been a real pain. I fully agree she needs to understand she can't keep putting things down toilets. We've had her do it here at home a few times and poor Adam's ended up taking the loo apart to clear the blockage (not his favourite job!).

Personally I find it completely infuriating when she laughs at being told off.

Tuesday, 13th December

Aggie - Today, after breakfast, Ruby suddenly handed me her lower front tooth. I'd never noticed it was loose when I cleaned them but then she's been a bit bite-y today and I was concentrating on keeping the same number of fingers I started with. So, she's a little gappy today but in a nice mood.

Hannah here, Ruby much better today (thank goodness). We had a lovely day for the children today with a trip to the theatre to see a panto which made them laugh a great deal. She was extremely well-behaved.

Ruby tired tonight; particularly because my sister took Ruby & I for a drive in the early evening. She was down for 9.30 and slept very well.

Wednesday, 14th December

Aggie - Singing from the moment her eyes opened; Ruby seems in the happiest of moods today...or she's planning something. If I sound paranoid it's because I'm feeling a little that way. She's quite cuddly but has been giving disconcerting little giggles for no particular reason I can find. I'm worried she's done something horrible and I just haven't found it yet.

Hannah here, Ruby and the other children have had a nice day finishing up all their cards and presents for Friday. There's been lots of hard work but everyone seems to have had a good time. Party clothes tomorrow, please.

Mellow Ruby tonight, she's been enjoying songs and games with Adam and I tonight. She settled late about 11pm and was quite restless until about 2am.

Thursday, 15th December

Aggie - Ruby very taken with her new party outfit and quite picky when she spilled a little cereal on it I had to carefully sponge it and reassure her that it still looked lovely.

I'm sending in a blue box and contents for you, Ruby's chocolates for the helpers and biscuits for the children.

Hannah here, BEWARE very large pins had been used to secure the table decorations and tinsel to tables today (I'm not sure who did this but I'm not happy about it) and several of these have disappeared. Knowing Ruby I thought she might have taken at least one but we haven't been able to find any I thought you would want to check for yourself to be sure.

Aside from that upset things have gone well and everybody's had a lovely time the food went down most quickly and we had a great party. Thank you for the lovely presents and cards particularly for my beautiful brooch, I'll treasure it.

Father Christmas is visiting us tomorrow! The children will be leaving early tomorrow home for 2.45.

No sign of any pins (thankfully) and I gather Ruby ate very well; she barely touched any food tonight and was yawning from very early evening.

Friday, 16th December

Aggie - Another pretty outfit for Ruby; she insisted on this to meet Santa. Her appetite has recovered and she polished off cereal, fruit and yoghurt for breakfast.

Hope you all have a very merry Christmas and a peaceful New Year and enjoy your very well-earned break.

Hannah here, Ruby looked lovely today and we had a wonderful time playing games and singing. "Daddy Cs'mas" was a huge hit with the children and it was lovely to hear Ruby name him herself. A very merry Xmas and New Year to you and I hope Ruby cooperates in making it an enjoyable family time for you all. Term commences on 5th January.

Christmas has been a bit lively with a bit of trouble for Ruby when cutting a back tooth she's had a lot of discomfort and developed a strange sort of nappy rash that became inflamed and sore. We had to get some medicine from the doctor and we used teething gel for her poor sore mouth. She even had earache that gave her a lot of discomfort and disturbed her sleep pattern. Despite this we've tried to give her a lovely first Christmas in our new home.

Ruby and Ivan had one set of presents at 7.30am with Adam & I. Around 9am my parents and sister came around with a second lot of presents and I served us all a special breakfast buffet. Ruby talked and sang a great deal we even succeeded in taping her singing "Jingle Bells" and added a speech by Ivan.

This is being sent to their great-aunt (my aunt Marian) who's a Carmelite nun in an enclosed order. She and her sisters rarely leave their house and she's never met or heard the children only seen their pictures. Her convent have been praying for Ruby's health since she was diagnosed with special needs.

Ivan's birthday went well too Ruby was able to join in (to some extent) with the singing and games without becoming too upset. New Year was a bit of a bother. Ruby had gone to sleep nicely and then all the ship sirens and horns went off for midnight, this sent the seagulls up into the air to wheel and scream overhead and they were shortly followed by Ruby who shrieked the house down. So we were up until 3.30am trying to get her settled again. Not my favourite way to see in a new year.

****

Thursday, 5th January

Aggie - Happy New Year! Ruby's in a really happy mood today and is obviously looking forward to returning to school. Ivan returned to school yesterday so she had an extra day with Mom & Dad to herself and made good use of this with a shopping trip. She's in her new coat and shoes today these are ones she chose herself and she's very proud of them!

Hannah here, Happy New Year to you! A lovely day lots of language here as well. Ruby seemed very happy to be back today and made a point of looking at all the toys, sitting on all the seats etc. Now let's hope that this horrible rain stops and the sun shines for the rest of the month.

Please can you complete the permission

slip enclosed allowing Ruby to travel on public transport on Monday.

So thrilled with her day she was still beaming when she got home. Ruby had a wonderful evening with us and has been saying a lot of names which we recognise as other children and adults from the class. She's very much part of the 'group' these days it's lovely!

Friday, 6th January

Aggie - Still very tired today but excited to have another day at school. She's eaten well and waited quite happily for the bus to come.

Hannah here, a good day today. Ruby has had sensory room and the computer in the am she's using the computer for number and colour matching. In the pm it was a makaton video for language work with practise of simple signs and their spoken versions. Last thing we took a walk around the shopping centre and had a nice time window-shopping their new displays.

On Monday we are heading to McDonald's on the bus and having lunch for Salim's

birthday. On the permission slip can you indicate what choices Ruby prefers or anything she's not allowed to eat.

A good weekend despite Ruby seemingly having at least one more back tooth cutting. Her 'rash' remains under control but the earache has been terrible for her I've taken the GP's advice and given her a little paracetamol and warm cloths to ease the discomfort for her.

Monday, 9th January

Aggie - Ruby appears to be excited about the prospect of a trip out for lunch! I'm sending the permission slip, card & present for Salim and an extra change of clothes for Ruby as I know what she can be like with tomato sauce. We don't do fast food very often so Ruby will enjoy the novelty and she's very fond of chicken in all forms.

Hannah here, Ruby very well-behaved in MacD, we had an excellent time although she really does love tomato sauce, doesn't she? There was rather a lot of it!

Chicken nuggets seemed to be favourite and she enjoyed those although we had to stop an alfresco attempt to relieve one of the other children of their burger when that looked tempting.

<u>Beware</u>, we seem to have some sickness among the children it was mentioned by two of the parents in their message-books when I read them.

She seems to have enjoyed her trip out. I'm glad you stopped her from pinching other people's food she's a devil for pinching when we're all eating at the table and I regularly sit her next to me because she's so quick she's whipped a choice titbit off poor Ivan's plate. We have to be very firm with her about only eating off her own plate and no snatching.

Ruby does enjoy tomato sauce; it's one of the ways I got her interested in drawing pictures. We sat and made 'edible art' with tomato sauce, squeeze cream and cream cheese to draw pictures there were no worries if she sampled the 'paint' and it was pretty easy to get stains out.
A good night and down for a delightful 9.30pm so Adam & I got an early night. Bliss!

Tuesday, 10th January

Aggie - Ruby showing no sign of sickness; eating all before her and trying to persuade me to give her some of the chocolate Nanny sent over last night. She woke up in a good mood and looks set to stay that way.

Hannah here, thank you on behalf of Salim his mother reported he was thrilled with his birthday gift from Ruby. She, on the contrary, was a bit upset this morning (we think her temper was because she didn't want to work today for some reason)but she cheered up and became cooperative.

4 children away today and Gerry's party tomorrow.

Ruby does have a bit of a grump on, doesn't she? I had her "I can't" phrase a few times when I asked her to do things. I'm wondering if she's just testing limits to see what she can get away with. Late night (11.30) and restless but did settle eventually.

Wednesday, 11th January

Aggie - I've compromised on Ruby's outfit I don't think the weather's suited to party dresses so she's got a pretty top but nice warm trousers and a couple of extra changes.

Hannah here, Gerry's party went very well. The children had a lovely Mr Blobby bouncy castle which was a great hit. They ate beefburgers and chips with birthday cake to follow that was only served when they were finished on the bouncy castle as we thought it might get messy otherwise. A shame a few of them had to miss the party but this appears to be a nasty little bug.

Ruby appears to have had a good time she's picked at her tea and been in a very playful mood all evening. In bed before 10pm and slept well.

Thursday, 12th January

Aggie - Very early start to the day; seagulls woke Ruby and she was crying and refusing to be comforted. We brought her down for

5.30am and she's been going ever since.

Hannah here, if you hadn't mentioned it we wouldn't have known that she started the day so early she's been a live-wire and into everything. We've had some lovely painting today.

Tired by the time she got home and we had a drive out with my sister so soothed Ruby down nicely she fell asleep as we drove home and didn't really wake up when I changed her and put her to bed.

Friday, 13th January

Aggie - Very sunny disposition after her good sleep and she's all smiles for everybody. Is her swimming costume still fitting her correctly? Because everything else seems to be up a size recently and I think it may be time for a new one.

Hannah here, I should have mentioned that Ruby needed a new costume but I'm afraid it slipped my mind. We're going to have sessions at the Hooper Centre swimming pool for the next three weeks and it'd be nice if you could sort one out

for then. Her old one fits but it's getting just a little tight. Hope you have a good weekend.

Oops! Should have asked before now. I'll do my best to get another Minnie Mouse costume but I may have to settle for something else. I haven't been able to go this weekend as Ruby caused an accident by slipping by Adam and opening the kitchen door as I was pulling something out of the oven. Unfortunately in my rush to prevent her reaching anything dangerous I splashed oven fat on my feet and I've burned myself a bit and can't wear shoes because of blisters. I can't send Ruby with Adam as he wouldn't be able to change her since men's public toilets don't have that facility. I'll sort it out as quickly as possible.

Otherwise it's been a good weekend apart from Ruby continuing to have trouble with that back tooth she's cutting we've been using bonjela to help. To keep her cheerful I cooked her favourite food (rainbow trout she's got sophisticated tastes our Ruby)for Sunday dinner and she ate two whole ones a record even for her.

Monday, 16th January

Aggie- Ruby full of beans today and she's been laughing and playing games from first thing. I'm sending in a new towel and robe and her new costume will follow as soon as possible. My sister and mother have offered to take her shopping as my feet are still unable to bear shoes as yet.

Hannah here, very good swim with Ruby. She did seem a little uncomfortable with the costume but it was just a bit of irritation from the straps. It's kind of your family to help when your poor feet are in such a state!

Today Ruby was swimming (with armbands) from the middle of the pool to the side and she showed great confidence in the water.

Clever Ruby; she's not like her Mom, who only managed to learn how to swim when she was 22! Lovely mood tonight and she was asleep for 9.30 and slept steadily through the night.

Tuesday, 17th January

Aggie - Ruby very happy this and has lots of appetite today she's been eagerly looking out for the bus from very early. I'm sending in the new costume my sister & Mom picked out it's not Minnie but has very pretty flowers which she seems to like.

Hannah here, Ruby looked gorgeous in her new costume and preened when we complimented her! She does love to be the centre of attention, doesn't she? Very good swimming today.

Tired again tonight; I like it! She ate tea, played a little and then demanded a story (most unusual for her) and fell asleep after only a couple of minutes. Slept very well.

Wednesday, 18th January

Aggie - Ruby in a bit of a grouch today; did not want to get up. Her swimming things never came home to be washed/dried, do you have anything for her? I'm sending a back-up costume/towel/robe just in case.

Hannah here, sorry, I should have mentioned we thought it unfair to keep asking parents to wash & dry swim-wear overnight and we used the washer in the nursery to get things ready. The back-up swim things are appreciated in case of 'accidents' anyway. Another good session at the pool.

Thank you for the reassurance, and for saving me washing! Glad Ruby's having a good time. Nice and relaxed sleep tonight.

Thursday, 19th January

Aggie - Not so happy today; she's been a bit 'offish' and inclined to throw a tantrum about nothing much.

Hannah here, I'm afraid Ruby refused to go into the water today. She was very difficult about getting changed, finally did and then stripped at the water's edge and threw her costume in the water. We took her back to the changing room's to dress again and she sat playing with a helper until the end of the session. I'm not sure what's caused this reaction, I

hope nothing that we've done, but we'll try again tomorrow.

Sorry to hear about Ruby's acting out. It's so hard to understand when she suddenly turns against something she's enjoyed but we've seen her do similar things before. I'm quite sure it's nothing that you or the other staff have done sometimes Ruby just does these things and we have to cope as best we can.

Friday, 20th January

Aggie - Slightly better mood today although I don't think her quality of sleep was much last night (that darn tooth). I've talked to her about the swimming and she's doing her 'blank' face and ignoring me.

Hannah here, another failure today I'm afraid. Ruby refused point-blank to get changed and actually threw herself on the floor and drummed her heels. We kept her there until the end of the session but she deliberately turned her back on the water and was very restless.

If you're happy about it I think we should discontinue the sessions for Ruby she

doesn't seem to be enjoying herself and the place could be used for another child who would. Do you agree that's reasonable? If Ruby changes her mind we can offer her another chance but I don't feel it's fair to her to make her take part in something that seems to be upsetting her. Let me know what you think for Monday, have a good weekend.

If you agree with me then can you please send extra PE kit and I'll organise some 'gym time' to give her a fun alternative.

Thank you for letting us decide for Ruby, Hannah. Adam and I have discussed it with Ruby (as much as we could) and between ourselves. We agree that it's for the best to give another child the chance if Ruby isn't getting anything from the opportunity. We've explained to Ruby she won't be going again unless she asks.

I have to say Ruby's general behaviour this weekend has been appalling not only has her sleep pattern been non-existent but we've had several episodes of wetting the floor or chairs. We even had another 'dirty' episode in her bedroom which was quite horrendous. There have been no diet or environment changes so we think it's just unfortunate; sometimes Ruby just goes through spells when she's very unhappy, unfocused and, frankly, pretty ghastly to live with.

I think getting her own way about swimming has pleased her because since we had the discussion with her she's seemed happier and more pleased with life.

Monday, 23rd January

Aggie - Ruby's very definitely in a better mood now she knows she's not going swimming. We've explained that she'll get to do exercises instead and she's been beaming at us and generally seems a lot happier. I think it's the right decision for her.

Hannah here, yes, it seems Ruby is happy. She found she would have the chance to take part in exercises and a dance class and was beautifully behaved throughout. Very smiling and relaxed. I'll keep her swimming things at school for use in the hydro tomorrow.

Parents evening on Thursday I have a cancellation and wondered if you would prefer to attend at 7.30 rather than 8.30? Ruby might be less tired and give you an easier time. Are you feet up to shoes yet?

The change seems to have pleased Ruby. She came home and when I asked her about doing exercises and dancing she proceeded to try a somersault (succeeded with help) and did some stretching. She asked for a music tape and was jigging about so Adam and I joined in. She found this hilarious and laughed so much she had a slight 'accident'! Good sleep tonight, only a couple of disturbances.

Tuesday, 24th January

Aggie - Ruby obviously looking forward to her day; tried to dress herself today and only let me help when she got in a tangle.

7.30 sounds fine to us and we'll be bringing both children so expect lots of questions from Ivan he's 8 going on 28 and quite the grown-up. I'll be interested in your reaction once you've met him properly. My feet are fine now; I'm lucky I heal quickly.

Hannah here, Ruby's had a good day. Very happy with new arrangement and seems to be enjoying mixing with some 'new' people.

She does seem happy and we can't help but feel it's a positive sign that she's enjoying time with unfamiliar people. She's always found that difficult and we're hoping it's a sign she maturing and perhaps becoming more social in outlook. It would be nice.

Wednesday, 25th January

Aggie - Poor night's sleep and she had little appetite for breakfast. I did wonder if she was incubating a cold but with her poking at her ears and biting me when cleaning her teeth I now think it's another tooth coming. Poor child goes through torment cutting each one. Do let us know if she has problems today.

Hannah here, I suspect you're right about a tooth she has been quite 'uptight' this pm. She certainly hated the new sounds that Alan's discovered and keeps making.

She did cheer up during her sensory

room session and we had interested (concentrated) work from her today. Hydro tomorrow.

Definitely a tooth; she was poking her ears and crying so I've rubbed her gum with bonjela, given a bubble-bath (always a treat), some pain-relief and auntie took us for a drive. When Ruby became more comfortable she started smiling again.

Later she was obviously in pain and distress so Adam and I alternated carrying her cuddled to us up and down the living room (no longer an easy thing to do with her latest growth-spurt!) until about 2am when she was finally able to settle.

Thursday, 26th January

Aggie - Ruby brighter today, although tired from her late (and painful) night. She was smiling when I reminded her about hydro today and that we would be seeing you tonight. We think the tooth must be easier because she's leaving her ears alone and has stopped biting everything (including me fortunately).

Hannah here, Ruby had a good day today she is quieter so perhaps her tooth has settled down. Today she's had singing, games, writing & hand control, jigsaws, play-work and sponge painting. A very busy day. Look forward to seeing you all tonight.

Both Ruby and Ivan tired in the taxi and she fell asleep shortly after he did so Adam and I had a quiet evening after 10pm. It makes a nice change!

Friday, 27th January

Aggie - It was nice to get all your feedback on Ruby and I did warn you about Ivan! He's astonishingly grown-up sometimes and interested in everything. Ruby a little dreamy today but seems very happy and let me clean her teeth without biting today.

Hannah here, Ivan is even more of a 'character' than his sister, such a pleasure to talk to! It felt a little bit like being interviewed and I almost felt I should pull out my cv for perusal.

A good day for Ruby I think she may have had earache and I kept her in at lunch-time she seems happy enough. Today was computer work & expression (sign & say work), sensory room, singing and free choice.

I took a look and confirmed it looked like another tooth was starting to come through that makes her sixth! It's been a poor weekend she's had little appetite and has been very disrupted. We've been using the nursing her in our arms to get her to sleep and making use of gel and pain relief. Even her skin is giving her problems as it's very acid as it frequently is when she's teething.

Monday, 30th January

Aggie - Ruby in a lovely mood; earache that her teeth cause seems to have eased a lot and she's smiling again. Another tooth at front came out today and we can't find it - I've a dark suspicion she swallowed it but we don't know for certain, it's just gone. At least she has some relief at last and we're just hoping it lasts for her, poor girl.

I'm hobbling a bit at the moment as I've got my feet sorted and now seem to be developing rheumatism in my right hip - honestly, I'm falling apart!

Hannah here, Ruby came in with a lovely mood but unfortunately this deteriorated and she became dreadful as the morning went on lots of screaming & wanting her own way. It may have been her ears/ teeth again as she seemed genuinely upset. Ate a good lunch and then was fine this pm.

Good mood continued when she came home. I think she was having some discomfort but seemed to be managing it better. Restless sleep but she did manage a reasonable amount.

Tuesday, 31st January

Aggie - Although Ruby is being a lot more difficult to handle sometimes (we're still getting some sleep disruption & generally very destructive) last night's good mood continued into today and woke up quite happy. I hope she'll have a better day today.

Hannah here, what a change! Ruby excelled herself today wonderful language use & excellent behaviour. Did you give her a 'happy pill' today? I'm on a course tomorrow (I knew it was too good to last) and Gail will cover for me.

If there was such a pill I certainly would! She's obviously feeling better right now and I wish it could last she's definitely got 6 teeth coming at once and I'm just hoping these finish coming through without too much further pain and she doesn't have any more for a while. Better sleep tonight although restless.

Wednesday, 1st February

Aggie - Lovely mood today although she's poking at her ears a little. I've used some bonjela and hope that staves off any further upsets.

Gail here, Ruby has had some discomfort today (fiddling with her ears) but has coped well and done some lovely singing and cutting-and-sticking today.

Not such a good night; she became quite

agitated and we had another night of carrying her up and down the room to nurse her to sleep. Finally settled about 1.30am and got to bed. My hip is aching like mad.

Thursday, 2nd February

Aggie - Ruby seems a little easier today and is quiet but has smiled a lot more and eaten a good breakfast.

Hannah here, no hydro today problem with heating so we'll have a session tomorrow when it's fixed. Instead we went on a walk and collected colours we're making a collage of colours and shapes from 'discovered' items.

Friday, 3rd February

Rubie had a very good night last night. Went to bed before 11pm. Sorry to be brief but this is Adam writing. Aggie is flat on her back right now poor old dad!

Hannah here, I hope Aggie improves soon do you know what's wrong with her? Let's hope she's up-and-about in time to

build a snowman. Work on snow today as the children find the recent fall FASCINATING. Well, it is rare here.

Monday, 6th February

Very happy girl in the main although ratty towards the end of the night. Woke this am in very good mood.

Aggie says thanks very much, starting to improve slowly. Too damn slow for Dad's peace of mind still never mind. Have fun in the hydro. Rubie's costume was/should still be at school

Hannah here, glad to hear Aggie improving. Ruby fine today seems happy enough and still enjoying our unusual weather. We're having another themed day on Wednesday so could you send any spare teddies you may have in with Ruby?

Tuesday, 7th February

In a rush, Rubie fine.

Hannah here, thank you for the teddies

Ruby has played with them all day.She and the other children have been enjoying 'The Very Hungry Caterpillar' book today as we're using it as the theme for our assembly on Friday.

Wednesday, 8th February

Hannah here, Ruby fine today. Hydro tomorrow Ruby will play the butterfly on Friday could she wear a pretty frock please?

Thursday, 9th February

Rubie not too well today got a bit of a cold still sweet enough temper if you have problems please let me know.

Hannah here, no hydro today too many 'sick' children (& staff) I'm afraid.

Friday, 10th February

Hannah here, Ruby looked lovely as the butterfly. I hope Aggie is feeling better soon. Please can we have a pair of wellies for Monday we're going on a nature walk and it's likely to be wet.

Have a good weekend.

Monday, 13th February

Sorry, no wellies. I tried to get some over the weekend but they do not seem to make her size any more. A pair of her old shoes are in her bag together with a change of socks etc in case they're needed.

Hannah here, I'm afraid Ruby got thoroughly soaked on our walk although she did enjoy herself. We dried and completely changed her and we've washed the things here to save you work while you're looking after Aggie. Any news yet?

Tuesday, 14th February

Have a good Red Nose day, I've put a £1 in Rubie's bag. She seems to be in a very good mood.

Hannah here, fun for everyone today with lots of fund-raising activities for Red Nose day. Ruby has had a wonderful time and seems tired so I hope both of

you get some sleep with her tonight. It'll be nice when things go back to normal tomorrow all this excitement is exhausting!

Wednesday, 15th February

Rubie fine today.

Hannah here, Ruby worked on photographs & symbols today with cutting-and-sticking, singing and doll play. She has been very happy today. Hydro tomorrow.

Ruby has answered her name on the register all three times this week (a first for us!) - she says very clearly, "Yes, here today."

Thursday,16th February

Hannah here, Ruby had a good hydro session today. She's been very happy and is generally giving good, clear responses to questions in class.

Friday, 17th February

Have just seen your comment re register: very impressed! Aggie starting to get better at last.

Hannah here, I'm glad you're pleased by Ruby's progress. She's had an excellent day today and been a real joy. It's good to hear Aggie is on the mend and I hope you both have a good holiday with her.

Hi, back to me, Aggie, commenting. I know why Ruby was so nice at school! She was saving all her 'horrid' for the holiday; she's really been vile at times, there's no other way to describe her. I know she's still having some problems with cutting teeth so the tantrums are no surprise but her behaviour's been so bad we can only put it down to my being laid-up in bed.

Ruby has developed a passion for oranges at the moment they've always been popular but she's being obsessive just now and we no sooner fill the fruit bowl than they're gone again.

Monday, 27th February

Aggie - Ruby's full of the joys today but Adam's driven demented chasing after her as I'm no help at all still right now. She's eaten a large breakfast and said "school" half-a-dozen times and is really excited.

Hannah here, are you feeling better now? Adam mentioned you were recovering. What happened? He's been so busy I didn't like to press for an explanation.

Ruby settled to work very well today continued answering at register time and read, "biscuit/drink please" so she's expanding her vocabulary. Hydro tomorrow.

If we can help in any way don't hesitate to ask.

Ruby in a very 'teasing' mood tonight. I'm afraid I fell asleep before she did.

Tuesday, 28th February

Aggie - Briefly; my 'rheumatism' in my hip was a disc blowing in my back - found my legs harder and harder to move until finally was unable to do so. Adam was out picking up Ivan from tea at my sister's and I had Ruby to look after. I had to put her in her bedroom and sort of block her in there once I couldn't move any longer and wait for Adam & Ivan to get home. Lots of pain and worry about why I was suddenly unable to walk and I had to chat reassuringly to Ruby whilst having a good sob into a towel I'd managed to grab. Adam came home and got me to bed.

I've seen the doctor and he's said it may improve with rest so I'm stuck in bed for the next few weeks! I'm about as much use a plaster on a wooden leg right now. If it wasn't for my parents and sister I don't know how poor Adam would manage.

By 'recovering' I think Adam meant 'in less pain', I'm on rather strong pain relief right now and can barely manage to get up for the loo. I can't sit for more than a few moments and standing is agony so lying down is the least painful option right now.

Thanks for the offer of help we may well need it!

Gail here, Hannah called to emergency meeting this am so I'm covering for her. I'll pass the information onto her when I see her. So sorry to hear about all your problems. Did the doctor explain what caused it?

Ruby was wonderful in the pancake races today and won a prize! She seemed disappointed that this didn't include eating the pancake, though!

Mom came to my rescue tonight and provided pancakes for the children since I'm unable to stand long enough to cook. Ruby more than made up for any that she missed at school!

Wednesday, 1st March

Aggie - Ruby really playful today and in a lovely mood. I'm due for another visit from the doctor today for him to assess my progress.

Hannah here, Ruby's done some good work today excellent object/symbol

matching, nice language use and singing. Hope doctor has good news!

She came home chattering away tonight I've never heard her so talkative. Kept poor Adam on the go until gone 10pm.

Thursday, 2nd March

Aggie - Ruby a bit tired today (after keeping Adam up half the night I'm not surprised) and rather dreamy. Not good news from doctor I'm going to have to be admitted to hospital for a couple of weeks to 'stabilise' my back. He thinks this may relieve the pressure that's causing me pain and weakness. Personally I think the weakness is from being stuck in bed for weeks at a time!

Hannah here, sorry to hear about your need for hospital stay. Will your family be able to help Adam? Ruby can be such a handful he should have some help.

The class is working on a new theme at present we're looking at dinosaurs! Ruby enjoys looking at pictures of them and makes a 'rawr' sound as she does. We're

going to be drawing pictures and making collages next week.

Adam said Ruby continued making her 'rawr' sound at a rather puzzled Fleur who seems to have taken it in quite good part. Not such a bad night asleep by 9pm

Friday, 3rd March

Aggie - Ruby's been making us laugh with her antics with Fleur she keeps stroking her and listening to her tummy as if she can hear something. We wonder if she's listening to gurgling noises from digestion.

Hannah here, Ruby does do some strange things sometimes it makes us smile too. Her language is so lovely these days she's asking for so much more it seems as if it has meaning for her now. Have a good weekend

It has been a good weekend and Adam and I agree with you that Ruby seems to be using language as if it means something to her now. She's had another breakthrough because while I've been ill she's started going to my sister's house again to spend time with her and my parents (giving poor Adam a break). Ruby's now fine with their dog, Jess she even fed her some chocolate. That was a big step forward. It probably helps that Jess isn't inclined to bark she's a big, black (we think) Labrador cross who adores people and children in particular. Sort of like a teddy bear turned into a dog.

Monday, 6th March

Aggie - Ruby singing today and petting Fleur again. She's in a wonderful mood and we're hoping this keeps up.

Hannah here, glad Ruby's cooperating in giving Adam a break he must need it! Today Ruby worked on counting, listening skills, singing, painting and cutting skills. Lots of concentration.

Nice night tonight asleep by 9.30.

Tuesday, 7th March

Aggie - Overslept today (I find it difficult to set the alarm) so Adam a bit rushed but he says

Ruby's fine. Apparently I'm due to go into hospital on 22nd of this month.

Hannah here, Ruby had a bit of a tantrum at lunch-time. Ate very little. It may have been her teeth again certainly nothing we could get to the bottom of!

Grouchy tonight and giving Adam lots of trouble my sister took her for a drive and brought back our usual cheery Ruby. Asleep for 10.30pm. A good night's rest for poor old Dad!

Wednesday, 8th March

Aggie - Ruby happy today so hope there'll be no repeat of the tantrum.

Hannah here, well, no tantrums but Ruby spent lunchtime running into the classroom and taking her clothes off! Not sure if the nicer weather is bringing this on but we've kept reminding her she's a big girl now and mustn't do this.

It may be the weather she's started whipping her clothes off whenever Adam takes his eyes off her. You'll just get a shout of, "Ruby! Put your clothes on!" from Ivan as he storms out of the room.

Thursday, 9th March

Aggie - Ruby's in a pensive mood today but very cuddly (which is pretty 'ouch' right now but I'm not going to say no to her) and has been stroking Fleur. When doing this she started giggling and then full-blown laughing as she looked at Fleur's tummy. We took a look and realised it was moving (a very 'Alien' moment I promise you, creepy!), poking her a little we realised the weight Fleur has gained recently has a rather obvious explanation - she's pregnant. So kittens at some time in the future and with Adam's luck it may be whilst I'm in hospital!

Hannah here, exciting news about your cat I'm sure Ruby will be thrilled to have kittens to play with. I wonder if she was listening to the kittens when you described her pressing her ear to Fleur's tummy?

Not so many 'strips' today. Playing in the sand-pit at lunchtime and she loved that!

Don't forget, teacher training day tomorrow. We'll see Ruby on Monday.

A good weekend apart from Ruby developing a niggly little cough something else she gets when teething I'm afraid. She's asked for and successfully used the toilet three times over the past couple of days. Brilliant!

Ruby also learned a new word "kittens". Fleur delivered two lovely, healthy kittens on Saturday 1 tabby & 1 black. It was rather funny; Fleur's never been a clever cat but pregnancy seems to have greatly puzzled her. On Saturday she went to use the cat-litter and promptly delivered her first kitten - a long, skinny tabby sausage that she cleaned but then abandoned in the litter, poor little scrap. Adam set up the box we had ready for her and transferred kitten One to there Fleur returned and promptly delivered the second kitten which she totally ignored. Adam had to cut off the after-birth as she started feeding the first kitten and continued to ignore the second. We succeeded in settling her down enough for kitten Two to start feeding.

After a few hours Adam brought Ruby in to see them she wasn't too sure what they were until they moved and then she was thrilled. We taught her to say 'kittens' and it's been her favourite word ever since!

Monday, 13th March

Aggie - Ruby very happy today she wanted to see the kittens as soon as she woke up. They seem to have her completely captivated. Her cough seems a little better today.

Hannah here, Ruby said "kittens" most of the morning! Her cough has not been too bad this pm generally she's been in a happy mood all day. Hydro tomorrow.

Bit of an upset with Fleur; had to call the vet in as she seemed poorly and it turned out she'd had a third kitten she failed to deliver. Vet's given her something to help delivery and advised us to keep an eye to her. We've kept Ruby's visits to a minimum to avoid any upset.

Tuesday, 14th March

Aggie - Fleur delivered the third kitten overnight - dead I'm afraid. Adam hid it away to avoid upsetting Ruby who had to make her morning visit. Fleur now seems to be doing better and Ruby is fascinated to watch them feeding.

Hannah here, shame about the kitten but Ruby had a happy day today she managed to stay on the playground for the whole of the breaks without running in to the toilet all the time.

Petting Fleur and kittens tonight was an on-going project, up-and-down the stairs all night to look and touch them. She's astonishingly gentle with them and becomes very giggly when they nuzzle or paw at her.

Wednesday, 15th March

Aggie - Ruby really happy today; very playful. She still has that cough so Adam's wrapped her up very warmly to ensure she doesn't get chilled and make it worse. We're so glad Ruby's being more cooperative we've noticed that presently, if she has to wait for something from us, we don't seem to be getting anywhere near as many tantrums.

Hannah here, Ruby did some good work today we decided to give her something

related to kittens and she's been loving cutting-and-sticking pictures of cats & kittens.

By any chance has she been tearing rather than cutting pictures today? Because she started ripping out pictures of kittens from a magazine and seemed puzzled when we told her off. Otherwise a good night.

Thursday, 16th March

Aggie - Lots of excited babble about the kittens, she's excited to see them a little more because Fleur's started wandering off to groom herself and leaving them to fend for themselves. Ruby was obviously worried they would get cold and was trying to cover them with a pillow. Had to explain that wasn't good for them although she was very kind to try to keep them warm.

Hannah here, Ruby not in a good mood today 2/3 tantrums but she calmed down a bit this pm.

Sorry to hear she's been ratty. All sweetness-and-light for us tonight, although poor Adam kept on the go bringing her up and down stairs to see her 'kittens'.

Friday, 17th March

Aggie - We're not sure what's got into Ruby but she's bouncing about everywhere today; seems most hyper. Hope she calms down.

Hannah here, Ruby in a bit of a temper this am (not sure what it was about) otherwise good and she soon calmed down. Loved her hydro session today, we had lots of giggles and dancing. Have a good weekend.

Ruby's cough seems to have developed into a real cold and we've had some sneezing over the weekend. I've been giving her medicine and she's stayed in very good spirits throughout. This is probably because of her captivation with the kittens we've been improvising lots of 'mom & baby' types of games with different toys. I've been teaching her the names for different types of baby animal eg kittens, puppies, cubs etc and she really likes repeating some of these and is increasingly matching the name to the type of animal. I'm very impressed!

Monday, 20ᵗʰ March

Aggie - Cold seems to have cleared for now and even the cough has stopped. She's got a good appetite again as well. Hope all goes well today.

Gail here, Hannah forgot to mention she was on a course today and will be back tomorrow, I'm covering for her. Ruby's been busy today lots of work around the numbers 1 and 2 this am and singing and painting this pm.

Ruby sneezing again tonight but her appetite and temperature are normal. She slept well which was useful as Adam is exhausted!

Tuesday, 21ˢᵗ March

Aggie - Ruby in a rotten mood I'm afraid. I've given her medicine just in case but no sign of cough or sneezes just lots of bad temper. Even the kittens didn't make her smile today.

Hannah here, Ruby stayed very angry on-and-off all day although we couldn't work out why. She's been quite prepared to

work (some good counting) but quickly becomes angry if you try talking to her and does her old trick of stuffing her fingers in her ears.

Wonderful Auntie Becca took Ruby for a long drive tonight and she came back in a much nicer mood although that may have had more to do with getting ice-cream!

Slept late (11.30) but good, solid rest.

Wednesday, 22nd March

Aggie - Ruby a little unsettled today; she's picking up that there's something going on I had to explain that Mommy won't be here when she gets home but that she'll be able to visit me in hospital where the doctors are going to make me better.

Hannah here, poor Ruby with so many changes happening she must be confused. We gave her an easy day with lots of free choice and she selected singing and painting which seemed to comfort her.

Monday, 24th April

Aggie - Here I am again, so much time has passed I don't know where to begin. Ruby's had a wonderful Easter (spoilt by everybody which she loved!) and made even more thrilling by the kittens' eyes opening and both of them gaining names.

First kitten (otherwise known as the tabby sausage) is now Hardy and second kitten is Laurel. We've named them this because Hardy is a rapidly growing bully who likes to whale the tar out of his brother/sister whenever he can get away with it. Laurel is a pudgy black softie who lets him/her get away with it.

Oddly enough Fleur who initially rejected Laurel now seems to dote on him and howls if they're separated. This is a problem as Laurel is so fat he's still dragging his legs and can't jump so when Fleur jumps up on my bed Laurel can't follow her, she then sits there and screeches for Laurel, Laurel howls for his mom and I yell for Adam to come put the two of them together because I still can't bend or lift and they're making me go deaf!

My less fun news is despite the hospital's efforts there's been no improvement and I'm down for a back operation in mid-June which may involve a spinal fusion. I've explained to my consultant that Ruby's had enough disruption and I just need to be back to functioning as a mother again instead of some kind of semi-invalid.

Ruby's in a nice mood and seems to be happy to have me home.

Hannah here, Ruby obviously feeling happy as she's been up to her old tricks a quick dash inside at lunchtime and she was stripped off and giggling before we could reach her. Very proud of herself too gave me the smuggest grin I've ever seen. Calmed down for the pm.

Sorry to hear about your impending operation. It's always a worry when you're facing something like that but I'm sure you'll be so much better afterwards but that doesn't help you now. We'll all be thinking of you.

Ruby also celebrated tonight by leading Adam a merry dance with one lot of mischief after another it was such a relief when she conked out shortly after 9pm.

Tuesday, 25th April

Aggie - Thank you all for your good wishes and I'm sure it will be worth the operation. Left to itself it can take up to a year to naturally clear and there's a high possibility it won't get better at all. I can't live like this if there's any way to get back to something like an active life again.

It's down for high UV today so I've sun-blocked Ruby and sent in the bottle in case more is needed later. You never quite know what Ruby will get up to next!

If you don't mind we'd like to skip parents evening this term I literally can't sit for longer than a few moments and standing quickly becomes agony.

Hannah here, don' t concern yourself about parent's evening, you've both got quite enough on your plate. I'll send

Ruby's lesson programme to you next week and you can just contact me with any concerns or questions.

No stripping today and a beautiful painting which she assures us is of her kittens. Apparently they're purple.

I could have guessed about the purple she came home with purple paint smudged on her skirt exactly where she usually smudges it onto my clothes. I guess when Mom's clothes aren't there to wipe her fingers she has to make do with her own. Little madam!

Wednesday 26th April

Aggie - Ruby horrible today spitting out food, stripping off clothes, screamed when I brushed her hair and when I turned my back (to get her clothes off the heater) kicked me in it.

If you have too many tantrums like this don't hesitate to call and Adam will bring her home I was in two minds about sending her in this sort of mood but she does appear to have calmed down after being told off for injuring me.

Hannah here, what a naughty girl! I do hope you've not been injured too badly?I think you had the worst of it before school. She has been fine in class lots of language.

Today we tried her with the microphone & speaker she was thrilled to hear her voice coming out of a box!

A different little girl to this morning. Whatever you did to calm her down please let me know! I wasn't injured, but it was- is- terribly painful and I don't want to be laid up in bed again. She's been rather cuddly tonight so I suspect she may be feeling guilty and trying, in her own way, to make amends.

Thursday, 27th April

Aggie - Hannah, I'm sending a copy of a letter which has been passed to me from our previous address near my parents. Apparently it was delivered after we had left the address and the flat has not been let since then so it's just sat there until the new manager carried out a spot-check on the property and contacted us. I'd appreciate your comments/advice regarding the contents:-

Lydia Bacardi,
Care Manager,
Children with Disabilities,
Seafront Social Services.

Dear Mr & Mrs Redd,

you may remember I wrote to you in February, shortly after I was appointed as Specialist Social Worker for the District.

I understand that after Ruby began to attend Upham School, Doctor Wyndham felt that she and yourselves might benefit from the advice and support of a Care Manager. As I have not heard from you I am assuming that you do not feel the need for such a service at this time. However, should you, in the future, wish to contact me for information on services etc. please do not hesitate to do so.

Yours sincerely,
Lydia Bacardi

Adam did try to contact the office in question and was told that Ruby's file has been closed, he's been left with the impression that we've pretty much been told to get on with it ourselves. Is that normal practice from your experience? It seems as if very little effort has been made to make sure we were happy with the decision just an assumption that if we weren't complaining there must be nothing wrong.

Hannah here, I'm not aware of having heard of anything like this before. I've always understood that no file was closed until every effort had been made to make sure that there was no existing need unmet. I can only suggest that you try to contact the office again and ask for assistance in your present difficult circumstances.

Ruby has been lovely today with lots of appropriate language and concentration on her number and symbol work.

Tomorrow's assembly is on the theme of favourite toys so could we ask you to send Ruby's current favourite toy not a kitten please!

Ruby very tired tonight and asleep for 7.30 but up again at 11pm then went through until 3am. Adam so very tired.

Friday, 28th April

Aggie - Ruby still quite weary (unsurprisingly) and is very clingy and cuddly today, not really her usual style these days as she seems to be enjoying being a big girl and more independent.

Hannah here, Ruby very good in assembly today. We used a teddy from the nursery for her to hold. Have a good weekend.

Ruby a lot happier this weekend as she's finally free of all trace of cough and cold. We've had lots of language and games and I finally managed to stand long enough to trim her hair it's not as neat as I'd hoped but all I could do in the time I could manage to stand for.

Monday, 1st May

Aggie - I do apologise for forgetting to send her toy on Friday, I'm afraid that these painkillers affect me more than I realise because it's not the first thing I've forgotten. Thank heavens for Adam reminding me what's needed (most of the time). Not sure what's wrong with her but Ruby's very ratty today; do hope she cheers up.

Hannah here, don't worry about, you've all got enough things to think about. I think Ruby was a little constipated today because she rushed into the class, used our toilet very thoroughly and went on to have a wonderful day - I'm returning a smiley Ruby to you today very happy. Looking forward to a good week heads down & get on with some work. Ruby has been great and everybody has commented on how good her language has been.

Thank you once again; such a pleasant change from this morning!

Tuesday, 2nd May

Aggie - Ruby a little ratty again to begin with but in a much better mood now- seems to have been the same problem again, she was bound up again for some reason. She's back to smiles again and I hope you have a good day with her.

Hannah here, we worked on counting, singing (with microphone, and Ruby likes to make a real 'performance' of her songs) & listening skills to everyday sounds in am. Singing practice with whole school & talk about spots (because we did stripes last week) this pm.

Bit of naughtiness tonight refusing to eat for Adam and making a big fuss about everything. Eventually settled down about 11pm but very restless sleep.

Wednesday, 3rd May

Aggie - Ruby threw a tantrum first thing but settled down quickly. Very good appetite and happy in herself again. I'm glad you mentioned about Ruby working on 'stripes' last week as it explains something she was doing. Last week she kept picking up Hardy and insisted on tracing all of his fur whilst saying "stripes." Now we know why!

Hannah here, more 'spots' work for Ruby

today, together with sensory room & singing. Ruby a bit 'uptight' this morning but not too bad. Hydro tomorrow.

A very good night tonight Ruby tired and asleep before 9.30pm.

Thursday, 4th May

Aggie - Ruby should be a bit happier today as she's had an immense bowel motion straight after breakfast. Afterwards she was back to her smiling self. I know it may seem silly but I've sun-blocked her today because I have a feeling we may be due for a scorcher today.

Hannah here, Ruby undid all your hard work (I'm afraid) with swimming today. Very naughty at lunchtime came into class, stripped and urinated all over the clean floor. Was I cross! No play for the rest of lunchtime she had to sit with me and hold my hand, which she did <u>not</u> like.

I checked to be sure and she hasn't done that since last September.

I hope this isn't a sign that we're seeing some of those other behaviours return! She's been very challenging tonight with lots of " I can't" and screaming. Late night almost 1am.

Friday, 5th May

Aggie - I've sun-blocked Ruby again and we've both emphasised how naughty she was yesterday. Honestly, we've had a few 'dirty' incidents of our own recently (usually at night) and we're only hoping it isn't a sign of her behaviour regressing. In case you need to renew her sun-block I'm sending in the bottle in her bag.

Hannah here, we sun-blocked Ruby after lunch & walk this pm. A quieter day no incidents at lunchtime and so we can hope it was a one-off occasion. I hope you have a good weekend.

A fairly good weekend in the main; she's had a couple of messy incidents but these may well have been involuntary. Otherwise she's been happy, using lots of clear and appropriate language and still very taken with her kittens. By the way, we've now established that Hardy's a male and Laurel a female but I'm not even trying to explain that to Ruby or she'll want to test if it works on humans!

Monday, 8th May

Aggie - Ruby in a jolly mood today she's been laughing and playing from very early today and seems to be ready to enjoy herself. Let's hope this sunny mood continues.

Adam and I are sorting out forms regarding Ruby's educational statement are there any points you think we should make or things to ask for? Previously we've found this to be yet another 'paper-pushing' exercise that has little effect but if you feel we may obtain extra resources for Ruby we'll try.

Hannah here, Ruby has been good & worked hard today although we've been having a problem with her kicking off her shoes (she seems to hate anything on her feet but in this heat so do I!)

I will get back to you if I think of anything that would benefit Ruby I can't think of anything at present. We're planning a trip out on Wednesday- I'm thinking the beach would be nice as it's some time since we've been.

As to her looking to see who's a boy and

who's a girl? I'm afraid Ruby isn't the only one who likes to strip in inappropriate places!

Ruby is insisting on bare feet at home but honestly, that's frequently how we all are inside the house. I've never cared to wear shoes other than where I had to and I'm afraid I've passed the habit onto both children Adam is the same.

A very restless night with this heat.

Tuesday, 9th May

Aggie - I've washed Ruby's hair to try to make her cooler and more comfortable. I've also sun-blocked her against this glare.

Hannah here, Ruby's had a lovely day. Today she's been shopping, had dance, music and sensory room. We thought a quiet day would be better in this heat.

Every door and window open and Ruby and the rest of us are still baking tonight. I've been lying down with Ruby by my side and been fanning her she seems to love the cool breeze, closing her eyes and moving her head around in the breeze.

Wednesday, 10th May

Aggie - Ruby has been sun-blocked and has pumps in her bag so that she can paddle in the sea. I've not been able to persuade her to wear any hat so I'll have to ask you to keep her to the shade wherever you can.

I've now been told that there's no hope of an operation before September at the very best, perhaps as late as next year. So I'm afraid I won't be any more mobile for the foreseeable future I don't think I'll be supporting the Summer Fayre this year.

Hannah here, sorry to hear about your operation being put off until September I do hope not any later than that. The sooner the better for all of your sake's.

Ruby had a wonderful time at the beach but did manage to get herself thoroughly soaked in the process. We've changed her clothes and kept the others to wash in the nursery washer, I couldn't let her go home in such a state.

I'm very glad you sent the sun-block I hope you don't mind that I used some of the lotion for a couple of others who were flushing in the heat.

What a thoroughly tired girl Ruby was when she came home! She yawned her way through tea, washing & changing and having a story. Fast asleep by 8.30 and stayed that way the rest of the night although disturbed by some noise.

Thursday, 11th May

Aggie - Ruby really ratty today the disturbance last night was some drunks fighting in the street on their way home from pubs or clubs. We ended up with police called and a lot of fuss ultimately it turned out somebody had been stabbed. Horrible.

No worries about using the sun-block it's for anybody who needs it in this sort of weather. Children's skin is so delicate and I hate seeing little ones burning in the sun as you sometimes do - you just know how much pain they'll be in later when their skin really feels the effects of over-exposure.

**Hannah here, we made jam sandwiches &
ate them out on the grass this pm. Ruby
thoroughly approved of the whole
process although she tried to speed it up
by grabbing a jar of jam and a spoon! In
a lovely mood despite the heat.**

She still came home and ate a good tea on top
of her lunch and sandwiches. Greedy girl.
Ruby's a bit of a devil for jam I have to hide
jars very carefully as she'll always go after
them with a spoon. "jam" is one of her
favourite words!

Very good sleep.

Friday, 12th May

Aggie - Ruby in a very good mood today and
seems to be looking forward to the day ahead;
she's been going to the front door with me to
look for the bus.

**Hannah here, I've been looking at Ruby's
progress in the class and I wondered how
you feel about her moving up later this
year? She's coped so well with
everything change of home, new class,
your illness and her kittens arrival and**

carried on doing such good work regardless. I think Ruby's ready for some new challenges and it seems that there are discussions about setting up a class for children on the autistic spectrum which could offer them special help and support. Would you and Adam consider that something Ruby would want and benefit from? Let me know what you think after the weekend.

Ruby's had a good day and done some excellent language and individual work.

A medium-good weekend; Ruby's been quite demanding of attention and has enjoyed getting Adam to do craft-work with her. There's been a lot of language use, most of it appropriate but we're still getting some strange uses as well; she's taken to shouting 'food' words when she's angry (like 'bacon' or 'ketchup').

One thing that's been amusing us recently is that Hardy is such a bully for being a tiny little thing now he's having solid food he growls and hisses at his mother and sister if they try to eat before him. The two of them have to wait until he's eaten his fill and then he moves away and lets them eat. Honestly, I always knew Fleur was daft but letting her own kitten bully her?!

Monday, 15th May

Aggie - Ready and raring to go today; Ruby is anxious to get to school today as she's been looking and asking for the bus since she got up.

Adam and I have been talking it over and we both think getting Ruby some help with her language and behaviour problems sounds like a good idea. We're just concerned that we don't want her to feel stigmatised by having to go into a separate class. You know Ruby very well do you honestly think she could benefit from moving to this class?

Hannah here, from what I've seen of the proposal this could be exactly what Ruby needs her new teacher is somebody with ten years experience of teaching pupils on the autistic spectrum, she makes use of the PECS (Picture Exchange Communication System) and the TEACCH (Treatment and Education of

Autistic and Communication related handicapped CHildren) training system. She'll have three classroom assistants who'll be especially trained to meet autistic spectrum needs. I think it has the potential to be a very good environment for Ruby to learn and develop. However, you are her parents and you know best what her emotional needs are and any choice of class will be based on the choices you make with Ruby's best interests in mind.

If I can give you any further help in making this decision don't hesitate to call and I'll be happy to offer any assistance I can.

Ruby's been a little monkey today lots of good painting, singing and PE but she's been 'pranking' us with that naughty twinkle back in her eye.

She lived up to the 'little monkey' title; clever Adam had found me a 'gripper' stick so that I can move around and lift things or pick up items I've dropped. Ruby' found a new use for it she was teasing all three cats by tweaking their tails and pinching their bums with the 'gripper' - fortunately not too hard. Both kittens seemed to enjoy the game but Fleur was less impressed and hid under the couch, hissing. Can't say I blame her.

Laughing was pretty painful but it was so funny to watch Ruby being consciously mischievous and amusing that it was worth it! She's quite the performer. Good sleep when she finally went down (10.30pm).

Tuesday, 16th May

Aggie -Nice mood today with lots of talking and play. Adam and I have talked it over and we think it sounds as if Ruby might benefit from the class but we'd like to know more about it. How would we organise finding out more details?

Hannah here, Ruby very interested in her symbol work today she was making up her own combinations and reading them correctly.

If you like I'll find out if it's possible for you to meet Marion, the autistic class teacher?

Not much of an appetite tonight but enjoyed a lovely long drive with Auntie Becca which gave poor Adam a break. Tired when she came home and asleep shortly afterwards.

Wednesday, 17th May

Aggie - We had one of Ruby's dreamy days she's been drifting off into a dream-world as we watched her. It's been awhile since we've seen this behaviour. Otherwise very happy just rather vague.

I'm not sure that I could make a meeting yet; I still can't sit for more than 5 minutes or stand for more than 20 before I'm in agony even with my painkillers-of-oblivion. I end up running with sweat with uncontrollable shaking in my hands it's not pretty.Adam could meet her on his own?

Hannah here, Ruby's remained 'dreamy' but has taken part in class. She's been quite focused during symbol work and singing but showed an inclination to wander in language. Not at all disruptive, she's cooperative, just somewhat vague.

I think meetings are being considered for late June/July is there any chance you might improve enough by then?

Ruby livened up when she came home oddly enough just when you'd have thought tiredness would have made her more sleepy. She does love to confound us. Late night and down for 10pm.

Thursday, 18th May

Aggie - More on the ball today; she's bright, lively and eating like a horse. Perhaps she's making up for yesterday's pickiness.

I truly don't know if I'll improve any further before my operation. I'm walking as far as the communal play area (about 100 yards) but when I'm finished I'm sweat-soaked and exhausted- end up lying on my heated pad to try to get the pain under control. It'd be nice to think that would change for the better but there're no guarantees.

Hannah here, Ruby her usual self today full of fun and games and ripe for a little mischief if she think she can get away

with it! Nice work in singing and language am with hydro pm.

I'll send you all the literature for the proposed class and you can judge for yourselves.

Somebody tired herself out because we had yawns over tea, eyelids closing in front of the telly and snoring about five minutes after we got her to bed (9.30pm). Adam looked in on her an hour later and she had snuggled so far under her covers that she had almost turned herself completely around and her feet were on top of her pillow.

She fiercely resisted being turned back so we compromised and folded back her duvet to make sure she could breathe.

Friday, 19th May

Aggie - Such a happy mood today; she's been positively beaming at everybody. You have to wonder if sleeping in the other direction suits her better for some reason? Maybe we should consider turning her bed the other way?

Good appetite and more independent than usual about dressing- which is why things took a bit longer because she was determined to 'get it right' and had to fasten/unfasten her shoes until they were correct. Or, she just liked the noise of the velcro fasteners.

Hannah here, excellent work of Ruby today singing & PE in the am, group and individual work in pm. Today she took the completed register to reception with help. Hope you have a good weekend

Every day she seems to take new step; we've told her what a 'big girl' she is and made a fuss of her.

In general a good weekend Adam and my sister took the children out for a trip to our local park where they could play, Ruby was loving having time on the swings until a couple of idiots decided to play piggy-in-the-middle with a frisbee and their noisy dog nearby. Once the frustrated dog started barking Ruby threw a major fit and they had to bring her home. It would be nice if you could guarantee places to take her that don't get barking dogs!

Monday, 22nd May

Aggie - All this lovely sunshine seems to

reflected in Ruby's personality because she's being just as sunny today all smiles and mellow attitude. She can sometimes be impatient if I take 'too long' getting her clothes or drying her after her wash, but not today. Ruby was chattering and singing as if she hadn't a care in the world. She's a real pleasure to be around on days like this.

Hannah here, I can see what you mean what a happy girl! Not only took the register but insisted on holding it with both hands (so not holding helper's hand) and handed it over with a big smile. Doing crafts today we're working on models in clay and papier-mache which will be dried and then painted later in the week. Ruby is making a kitten and seemed to love the texture of the paper she was squishing it between her fingers (we did have to watch her in case she decided to taste the glue).

Ruby LOVES papier-mache; Adam's very good with arts & crafts and he's done quite a few sessions with the children, one time he made a wonderful 'Green Man' mask that we dried and painted gold. Ruby thought that was wonderful and used to like to trace the features with her fingers.

A good, if late (11.30) evening and slightly restless sleep we were having noise in the street from some sort of party further down the road.

Tuesday, 23rd May

Aggie - Ruby's paying for her restless night I'm afraid; she's a bit bleary-eyed and although generally happy can get a little peevish from time-to-time. Not much appetite today but she had eaten some fruit and yoghurt.

Hannah here, all of the children were restless today for some reason (something in the air) so we decided to have an easy day PE in the morning and a long walk around the shops and local area after lunch. The models could do with some extra drying time and in one or two cases some running repairs. Ruby's rabbit keeps losing one of his ears and I've had to add some PVA glue to keep it attached.

She's certainly felt the benefit of all that exercise; Ruby asked for bed at 7.30pm and (to our surprise) went pretty well straight to sleep, staying that way even when some fool parked at the end of our drive with his windows open and radio blasting out at an almost painful level. We chased him off but this has become a regular problem now - they all seem to be visiting a house further down from us (the one with the ghastly little vandals live) but leave their cars outside our house. Probably because the chap that lives there seems to permanently have both his drive and the pavement filled with his own vehicles.

Wednesday, 24th May

Aggie - Well, we've had some 'fun' here today! When I went in Ruby's room to wake her up I noticed a police riot van going past our house but slowing down and stopping further down from us, two more police cars parked behind it (one of them outside our house) and a load of police officers in body-armour piled out of the van. I called Adam and we both moved to the landing to watch.

I'm not usually one for curtain-twitching but we were wondering what exactly was going on there was a lot of shouting and pounding noises which subsequently turned out to be the door of Mister-Three-Cars house being broken down. We had to break off watching to see to Ruby but snatched odd moments to see what happened. There were a few large metal boxes and black plastic sacks removed which seemed very heavy and a whole bunch of people were driven off in the police cars.

Hannah here, Ruby came in just as usual no sign of all your upset today. Did you find out what was going on? I was telling the others about it and we're all agog to know!

Our local area is rampant with gossip; apparently popular belief is Mister-Three-Cars has been dealing drugs and the big metal boxes were guns being confiscated. I'm hoping that one's just a rumour. I HATE guns! The very idea of them right on the doorstep no, definitely don't want that.

Ruby is still blithely indifferent; all she wants is her tea and games.

Thursday, 25th May

Aggie - Ruby's a bit excited because I've explained that we're having a little party tonight (she was fixated on 'cake'). I hope she'll settle down and not stay as distracted but she is rather over-the-top.

Hannah here, Ruby's stayed excited but has still settled in and done some good music, hydro and singing. Today we finished our models and Ruby's rabbit appears likely to remain two-eared for at least the foreseeable future.

Ruby tired out with our celebration and conked out nicely at 8.30pm only a little stirring when we had noise from the street again.

Friday, 26th May

Aggie - Grandad Walker's 70th birthday yesterday we had a lovely family party. Ruby sang "Happy Birthday"and then said, "cake!" Afterwards we got "cheers" when she toasted him although Ruby was most miffed and she and Ivan got bubbly juice instead of champagne. We pointed out that at not quite 7 & 8 for Ivan both of them were a little young for booze, not that Ivan has any interest but I get the impression Ruby thinks she's missing out!

With all the excitement she fell asleep at 9pm and slept through. We were so grateful!

Hannah here, it sounds as if you had a lovely time. Ruby's been full of comments about 'Grandad' and 'cake' and she gave us a sudden chorus of 'Happy Birthday' which had Gerry and some of the others joining in. They were most disappointed when we explained there was no birthday cake coming!

Have a good break.

It's been a good holiday Ruby a lot happier now she's free of her cough and appears to have stopped sprouting teeth (honestly, I think sharks have less than the poor child's been growing!). We've been having lots of appropriately used language and imaginative games.

Monday, 5th June

Aggie - Nanny Walker & Ruby's birthday

yesterday (it's hard to believe Ruby's now 7 and I'm not sharing my Mom's age or she'll tell me off!) and our family party went well, Ruby very taken with her new trampoline.

I was hoping to be able to hold a party for Ruby's class but not while I'm like this. Would it be possible for us to pay for the whole class to have a day out somewhere? I'd be very grateful if you could offer any suggestions of venues or any alternative suggestions if trips are too difficult to organise.

Hannah here, we'll gladly give Ruby a bit of a party in school if it will help you. We could do that this week if you like you could either send a cake (or money and we'll buy one) and any other food you wanted to. We'll leave singing 'Happy birthday" or giving her a card until 'party' day so as not to confuse her.

If you want to pay for a day out our next mini-bus day is 12th June next Monday but it's swimming and can get quite expensive. We can just take a cake with us, sing "Happy Birthday" and make the day a bit special that way. Let me know what you want to do.

Ruby in one of her strange moods tonight; she's not tired exactly but just not interested in interacting with us she prefers to stare off into space. You can win her attention for short bursts of time but she quickly drifts away again. It really does look sometimes as if she's listening or watching things we can't see or hear. Settled to bed reasonably early (9pm) but continued to talk/sing for a long while yet wouldn't go back downstairs.

Tuesday, 6th June

Aggie - Adam and I have discussed it and we'd really like to pay for a day out as Ruby's missed out on a lot of trips and treats because I'm still mostly confined to the house. (I really can't count Ruby walking around with my hobbling after her on a couple of sticks as much of a trip out for her). For next Monday we'll send in money, cake and a few snacks for them to share.

Ruby's thrown out a strange little rash on her arms today only her arms and no obvious cause. Other wise she's healthy (no temperature or itching) so I'm wondering if yesterday's new jumper irritated her skin, I've put on a soothing lotion and they seem to be fading. Call me to pick her up if she starts to show any other symptoms.

Hannah here, well , thank you and Adam. If you're both happy we'll take the children to Garthlands where they have the water-slide and other features. We'll take them there and have a picnic party afterwards in the park they love nearby. No sign of a rash now- your lotion must have worked. We'll keep an eye on her in case.

Just wanted to ask how Ruby is with the kittens? She's still talking about them a great deal and they must be getting quite big now.

Really good night; Ruby's new trampoline does seem to tire her out nicely but I'm so glad we got the version with a bar to hang onto my heart's in my mouth sometimes the way she throws herself onto it and keeps bouncing higher and higher. I'm glad the rash is gone, that was strange, but I can only put it down to a reaction to that top and I won't be using it again just in case.

The kittens are still very popular! Ruby may

be pouting after this weekend as Hardy will be going to live with my sister and parents we wouldn't dare separate Fleur from her beloved Laurel!

Wednesday, 7th June

Aggie - More fun & games today, but not with Ruby. Our neighbour, Mister-Three-Cars surfaced during the holiday as if nothing had happened and the front door was replaced. Today we had a riot-van, police cars, multiple officers and another raid with the door was bashed in again it looked like more arrests this time but fewer items confiscated from the house. Thankfully no more of the metal boxes.

Ruby's only reaction was when a police dog barked a couple of times when she crammed her fingers in her ears, hunched her shoulders and said, "bad dog!"

Hannah here, it's all happening around you, isn't it? At least Ruby isn't being disturbed (apart from the dog) but it's more than a bit frightening.

A little unfocused today but some good language & object/symbol work. Have

you and Adam given any more thought to Ruby's class?

Rather a fretful night so Ruby may have been affected by events this morning after all. She asked for bed early (8pm) and went to sleep but up again by 9.30 and awake until 1am.

Thursday, 8th June

Aggie - Adam and I have talked it over and we think your recommendation gives us greater confidence that this new class could work for Ruby. Do you need us to do anything?

Ruby has eaten a huge breakfast today; I'm not sure if she's used up more energy with her late night and has to replace it or if she's being outright greedy.

Hannah here, Ruby does seem hungry doesn't she? We did have hydro am so perhaps that built her appetite up. Today she took the register to reception on her own (with the helper watching from the class door, I promise) and Ruby was perfectly confident. She handed over the register, accepted a sweet (sugar-free) and returned to class

without any prompting excellent! We're very proud of her for being so 'grown-up'.

What a star! We've made a huge fuss of her and praised her immensely for taking such a step forward she's becoming so independent that it astonishes us.

Good sleep tonight.

Friday, 9th June

Aggie - Lovely mood today; Ruby full of smiles and still assuring us she a big girl. We've given her more praise and reminded her that she'll be singing "happy birthday" for real tonight because it's my sister's turn for a birthday (we do tend to cram them close together on my side of the family, don't we?). "Cake," Ruby said smugly and grinned at me.

Hannah here, you should have no problem getting Ruby to sing today as she's started several times today there were some disappointed children today because they seemed convinced cake had to be imminent this time!

Pretty good weekend with lots of appropriate language use and Ruby's been much better-tempered than the last few days. Hardy went with my sister on Friday (an extra present she wasn't expecting) and there's been no reaction from Ruby; she's seemed to enjoy that Fleur and Laurel are happy to pop on her lap and have cuddles something Hardy wouldn't allow before, the little bully!

Monday, 12th June

Aggie - Ruby very excited today as she knows she's going out. I'm sending her swimming gear and sunblock for afterwards (I've included lip-screen but please try to ensure she doesn't eat it - it's strawberry flavoured and she's rather fond). Her pretty frock is chosen for being easy to clean so don't worry about spills/stains Ruby always gets that and I refuse to stress over it.

Money, cake, snacks and extra cash for emergencies (like an unexpected price rise for entrance, or failing that a need for ice-cream!) are in the large carrier bag. In there is an extra present each from ourselves, my parents and my sister. Hope the day goes well.

Hannah here, the children have had a wonderful day. After we took the register (which Ruby handed in beautifully) we toileted and then packed everybody into the minibus. At Garthlands they each had several turns on the water-slide and played in both of the splash-pools and played in the ball-pool as well.

At lunch-time we gathered everybody up and headed to the park where we laid out the picnic lunch provided by school (and your snack selection which was extremely popular, particularly with Ruby) and brought out Ruby's cake. We sang her "happy birthday" and she blew out the candles then we settled everybody to eat.

It was a little like watching a swarm of locusts descend I don't think I've ever seen food disappear so quickly. However, everybody finally seemed to be satisfied so we gave them free-time to play on the equipment and then played some throwing-and-catching games. Ruby meanwhile made several demands

(you couldn't call it anything else but demands) and we finally sat her down and gave her two of the smaller presents but reserved the rest to send home by hiding them in the back of the 'bus.

By the time we got them back to school they were all tired and inclined to be cranky so we had a final quiet singing session for the last half-hour of class. I do hope you have a good evening with her and some good sleep as she's been yawning for some time now.

Ruby had a great time opening all her gifts up and making an immense mess. She insisted on opening everything before she even ate tea and was delighted with the toys and books. Poor Ivan was traumatised when she stripped off to put on her new swimming costume (I'm not sure who that came from as Ruby was so over-excited she started chewing and trying to eat her cards and wrapping paper). Early night 8.30 and only a couple of disturbances.

Tuesday, 13th June

Aggie - It's good to hear everybody enjoyed their day so much. Please thank everybody for

Ruby's wonderful cards and gifts, she appreciated them very much! She's still excited and a little bit hyper.

Hannah here, a quieter day after all the excitement of yesterday we've concentrated on symbol/object work & PE with hydro in the pm. They all seem a lot calmer today Ruby included.

I have news apparently there's been a cancellation and the hospital are offering me an appointment for Thursday. I could have this thing over and done with before we reach the holiday so we would stand a chance of having something quality time as a family again! I've said "Yes" of course; it's not like I want to be stuck hobbling everywhere on sticks and doped on pain-killers but I'm a little nervous. I know that if I have a spinal fusion I'll lose some flexibility and I've already been warned that I can't expect to go back to being able to do everything I used to.

Anyway, Ruby's had a good night and was asleep for 10pm and resting well.

Wednesday, 14th June

Aggie - We've had a lively start to the day as Ruby decided to tear down her curtains and prance about naked in full view of the road! We honestly hadn't heard a thing and wouldn't have known what was going on if our neighbour from a couple of doors away hadn't been kind enough to knock our door and warn us.

I got her washed, dressed and downstairs and Adam took a look at the damage to see what he could do.She's very pleased with herself despite being told what a naughty girl she's been.

Hope she settles down for you.

Hannah here, well you've had both your nice and nasty shocks in one night and day. It's wonderful news that you have your operation due so much more quickly than you hoped but you really didn't need Ruby pulling a trick like that! Thank heavens for your neighbour.

Honestly, if you hadn't told us how badly she'd behaved I'd never have guessed - if anything she's been particularly good

today. We've had lots of hard work, good concentration and she's worked hard to use some new words. Very much hope Adam can repair the damage and you have a better night before your trip into hospital tomorrow. Everybody wishes you the best and hopes for a good result from the treatment.

Thank you for the good wishes. Adam has done his usual miracle and managed to seal the wall and replace the pole (she hadn't just pulled down the curtains but yanked the screw-fixings for the pole right out of the wall). We've been able to replace the curtains but (knowing how Ruby repeats behaviours) we're very concerned that she'll just do it again. Time will tell.

I will be travelling in by ambulance tomorrow and expect to leave before Ruby does so I'll be back in touch once I'm home again to let everybody know how things have gone.

Monday, 3rd July

Aggie - Here I am, turning up like a bad penny! I've been incredibly lucky; no spinal fusion my specialist used a different procedure that will leave me (eventually) with an almost complete range of motion. I can now sit for short periods of time without agony, walk without stabbing pain and standing no longer makes my right foot go completely numb. I'm not pain-free but it's an awful lot better and I have a regimen of daily exercises I have to follow if I don't want to seize up again.

I'm assured that I will be able to bend in the near future (I honestly can't yet) and I have a follow-up appointment for three weeks time. Things are looking good - I just have to accept there are some things I can't do any more. No lifting Ruby, no bending forward (I have to kneel instead) and not pushing my walks beyond a distance where I'm mildly uncomfortable.

I had to fight to get sent straight home; the hospital and specialist wanted to send me to a convalescent home to fully recover. I told them I wanted to be home with my husband and children, thank you very much.

There were lots of stern warnings about not over-doing things or I'd undo their hard work and they sent me home in an ambulance. For whatever reason they had me travel back on a stretcher (with straps to prevent me falling out) and I was sharing with 3 other patients on their own way home. The ambulance stopped at one sheltered housing site and the two attendants took one patient (who was very elderly and frail) into the property leaving me fastened down and waiting.

Being friendly I asked the two people with me, "Just finished your treatment? Or are you day-patients?"

They looked at each other, then at me and the man said, "We've just been discharged. We met each other during treatment." Since they were sitting holding hands I commented, "That's nice. What ward were you on? I didn't know they still had mixed ones."

"We were at Fieldborne; Janice for depression and I was sectioned for observation after being arrested for assault. They dropped the charges and I'm on day-release now."

"Oh, that was lucky! And nice you got the chance to meet."

We chatted for a few more minutes until the attendants returned and we then drove to another sheltered housing site where the couple got out and waved goodbye.

The paramedic riding behind with me asked, "Are you feeling OK? You look a bit pale."

"Not really. Not for somebody strapped to a stretcher who was left with a former psychiatric patient who's recently been sectioned after being arrested. I was having a lovely chat with him and his girlfriend."

He looked a little shifty and laughed, "He was winding you up."

"He did a good job. Can I go home now, please? I was rather hoping to get back before the pain meds wear off."

When we arrived at my house it turned out the gas company had decided to dig up the road and pavement right in front. The two crew were just trying to decide how to safely get my stretcher past when I said, "Pass me the crutches - the physio said I had to walk a little every day and my front door looks about the right distance for today."

Hannah here, so good to hear that

everything went so well although your trip home sounds hilarious (if frightening), I bet it wasn't at the time though. Ruby's coped well with your being in hospital but we've had a few incidents. I'm hoping she'll settle back down now that she's got Mom back and on her feet (so to speak).

Today we've been working on language Ruby's been working with us to make her pronunciation as clear as possible, she's still using her trick of 'approximating' a word or sentence and repeating it gradually getting closer to the correct sound.

Yep, once I was home it was funny not so much at the time. Ruby's not quite sure about having me home right now. I think she's half-expecting me to disappear again and I'm having to be cautious about moving right now because all the nerves in my back are jangly and I tend to have some involuntary twitches and shakes when I get tired. Not a good thing if I'm carrying a cup of tea!

Ruby fine tonight; smiling and playful but not ready to settle until late (11pm).

Tuesday, 4th July

Aggie - Up with the lark today and about as tuneful; she's singing some tune that we vaguely recognise but neither of us can make out the words it's rather maddening, although even nonsense sounds good in her pretty singing voice.

Hannah here, we've had a very good day (I think Ruby is starting to settle down) finishing off some of the craft projects they've been working on this term Ruby will be bringing her work home on the 18th. Other than this we had language work in am and PE in pm.

She obviously enjoyed her craft today because Ruby insisted on having a painting session after tea; we had about an hour of her working pretty hard with Adam before she started to get silly and tried to paint Laurel (who's as daft as her mom and would have let it happen, I might add). After that it was games, TV and down to sleep for 9.30pm, a little bit restless with some of the late-night street noise but no real problems.

Wednesday, 5th July

Aggie - Rather reluctant to get up today; I still can't handle too much bending/twisting so when Ruby started to be awkward about getting up I asked Adam to take over. She was beautifully behaved then cooperating with washing, dressing and breakfast with no real problems.

Hannah here, I'm on a course tomorrow so Gail will be covering. Today Ruby's been working hard again individual work on symbols and numbers, singing in am and hydro pm. Marion is setting up meetings for parents whose children are transferring to the autism class in September they're going to be for next week.
Is there any chance you'll be fit enough?

Not sure what was wrong but we had a furiously angry Ruby when she came home tonight. She was ranting away to herself in a way that I've never seen her carry on before. Has something different happened? Very restless all night, poor sleep.

Thursday, 6th July

Aggie -Ruby calmer today; it's nice to see her back to her normal, smiling self. If you can't think of any reason then we're stumped! We've no idea what set off her temper but she was REALLY angry.

Yes, I think I could manage to make it to a meeting (although I won't guarantee to sit down for too long as I've a tendency to start hurting quite quickly) and it would help to chat in person. Could you set that up for us? Any day would suit.

Gail here, Hannah away on a course as she told you, I'm covering for her. Ruby's been fine today- whole class project on 'Summer' went well we've some lovely collages being put together- this am. PE and numbers in pm. I'll pass on your comments about meeting to Hannah when she returns. I've checked nobody here is aware of what might have upset her.

We had another outburst from Ruby tonight and she remained grumpy all evening. A late night (12) but finally peaceful once she went down.

Friday, 7th July

Aggie - Ruby happy again today; no problems at all. We may have an explanation for her outbursts of temper in the past couple of days one of the other pupils who's recently started using the bus apparently has a habit of compulsively whistling and making sucking noises. They're both things which drive Ruby crazy we have screaming tantrums if we forget and whistle or make certain noises. I'm not sure how we can address that issue; do you have any suggestions?

Hannah here, Ruby was in a temper when she arrived today I gather the same pupil was on the bus today. We have her calmed now and she's working well on objects and symbols. I've spoken to the school office and they'll arrange for them to travel on separate transport tonight and in future.

I've also arranged an appointment for you and Adam to meet with Marion on

Tuesday, 11ᵗʰ at 10.30am. I hope that's suitable but if not let me know and we'll try to arrange some other time. Hope you have a quiet night and an enjoyable weekend.

You're a miracle worker! Ruby was home a little sooner but in such a sunny mood that tonight's been a pleasure. Lots of talking and games with no sign of distress or anger so I think you've fixed her problem. Her happy mood has continued for the whole of the weekend and we had a lovely trip out on the Otter line train on Sunday.

You know what a huge fan of Thomas she is so the train instantly became "Thomas" and she was rapt. That's something we're going to try again lots of walking tired her out and we had a fabulous night of solid sleep.

Monday, 10ᵗʰ July

Aggie - In a lively mood today and she's been eating all before her (and before us we aren't careful!). Ruby's obviously keen for school because she's been checking for the bus since she got dressed.

Hannah here, using the different bus has obviously worked because Ruby arrived in a lovely mood smiling, happy and eager to work. We've had some very good singing and craft in the am and a class walk in the pm.

The walk must have worked as Ruby was unusually tired tonight she decided to settle at 8.30 and we half-expected to have her wake up again. She did need a couple of changes but went off to sleep again relatively quickly.

Tuesday, 11th July

Aggie - Lots of chatter and smiles today; Ruby's been talking about 'swimming' is it hydro today? She said it so clearly and insistently that we thought it must be something she's expecting to happen rather than a random comment.

Hannah here, yes, Ruby was time-tabled for hydro today in the pm, we had language work and painting in the am. Very good work and she's remained in a cooperative mood all day.

Very happy tonight; ate well and had games

until 8.30 then asked for bed. She was disturbed at 10 & 2am by street noise but otherwise slept reasonably well with three changes.

The meeting with Marion went well (I don't know if you had a chance to talk to her) and we had a good chat despite my having to stand up and walk when my back became painful.

It sounds as if using different trays to split up activities and symbols for her time-table might suit Ruby very well she's inclined to be happier and more focused if she knows exactly what's going to happen and what she's expected to do.

We make a point of explaining exactly what we want of her because Ruby's not good at working out what we're asking for unless we use really clear and exact language.

Both of us think your suggestion's a good one and we're very hopeful that Ruby will like the change and continue to flourish. (crossed fingers).

Wednesday, 12th July

Aggie - Lots of excitement here today; my sister came around very early to let me know it looks as if her car has been stolen at some time during the night. She drove into town and to the local shops yesterday so it must have been taken after that. Apparently Becca has to wait to speak to a policeman and was letting me know in case I needed a lift. It's horrible Becca drives my Mom everywhere and she's got her business to run, I don't know how she'll manage without transport.

In any case, Ruby was pleased to see Becca and has been in a lovely mood again lots of appetite (plus nagging Auntie for "sweets... p'wees.")

Hannah here, what a terrible thing to happen! I know your sister's always so good about helping with Ruby and transporting items for the school fayre. I do hope it's found quickly for her and not in bad condition she did have full insurance, I hope?

Ruby working on collage for Summer Fayre we're having a theme of 'holidays'

and she's been working on beach scenes as she loves painting and cutting fish and making the Makaton sign as she says "fish." We've noticed before that some favourite words Ruby still signs quite readily even though her language is clear enough to not require reinforcement with a sign.

That may be my fault; I still find myself signing to some old favourite nursery songs that we learnt together so I may be unnecessarily adding a physical element I blame it on all those late night sessions of singing where if I didn't keep some sort of movement I'd find myself dropping off.

Rather noisy tonight but very good-humoured, in fact full of old nick as Ruby's just looking for the chance for mischief. She's been pretending to sit on Laurel as that makes Adam and I panic it's noticeable that she doesn't pretend to sit on Fleur as her single attempt a few weeks back led to a clawed bum. I didn't honestly blame the cat if something as big as Ruby is to her tried to sit on me I'm pretty sure I'd lash out to drive it away too!

Down very late 12.30 but nice solid sleep.

Thursday, 13th July

Aggie - Ruby's been romping today; there's no other word for it. Both cats have decided to hide under the couch because she's been stamping and twirling about like a spinning top. Haven't seen her do that for some time she whirls and whirls until she's staggering around the place as if she's drunk. We've tried to calm her down with mixed success and Ruby remains VERY giggly.

Hannah here, Ruby was trying to carry on spinning here too. It may be that she's seen somebody else with this behaviour and its reminded her of something she used to like to do. It's obviously very absorbing because we had to persuade her to stop as she remained in a world of her own when twirling and it was disrupting others in the class.

However, once we got her past that stage she settled to some very good group interaction and language work in the am and PE with free choice (she picked

painting) when we had some visitors from the new intake in September.

The saga of Becca's car continues apparently the police found it last night when a local shop reported a vehicle parked in front of their premises. It seems that Becca drove there with Ivan (not sure why as it's very nearby to us) and when they left the shop the people who run it were puzzled to see them walk off and leave the car behind!

Becca says the police were very nice about it and told her it's not the first time they've had somebody do something similar just for her to next time check before reporting it stolen. I commented to her that she's always been an over-achiever, most people only lose their car keys but she can manage to lose the whole car. I received a look and the raised-eyebrow-of-doom which, oddly enough, both of my children seem to have inherited from her. You haven't been fully disapproved of until you've been 'eyebrowed' by my sister!

Friday, 14th July

Aggie - We had Ruby start again on spinning today so I resorted to distraction-by-bribery (otherwise known as "who wants chocolate for breakfast?"). I'm sure there's a special circle of hell reserved for mothers who give sweeties for breakfast but I'm prepared to risk it. I remember Ruby's spinning days and they weren't fun she could go for hours and wouldn't pay attention to anything else. I went all over the room hiding two or three smarties at a time in different spots and Ruby had to follow me around trying to find them. She had a whale of a time and just about pulled the living room apart hunting for her 'prey'!

I did squeeze some nutrition in there too she had yoghurt and fruit with a carrot afterwards to clean her teeth as I wasn't feeling brave enough for a second round of biting. Tomorrow I'll have a non-calorific distraction ready in case she starts again.

Hannah here, considering we have one child here (not in my class fortunately) whose only accepted solid food is a specific chocolate cake and nothing else I wouldn't worry too much. I know she loves her fruit and veg so perhaps you could hide berries or baby tomatoes if you're worried about her teeth?

Your distraction worked because we've had no spinning today lots of excellent object/symbol work with singing in the am and a long walk to the shops as it was so stifling in our classroom. Ruby will be bringing all her work projects for the year home on Monday and we've booked a mini-bus trip for the day as a special treat. Please complete and return the permission slip for Monday and have a good weekend.

Not the greatest of weekends; Ruby's been inclined to be tearful which may be because she realises school is coming to an end soon. We've been describing the days out we want to have with her and the things we'll do to try to reassure Ruby that things are still fine. It's such a shame that every time her routine changes it seems to take so much of her sense of security away.

Her sleep has been disrupted but not too bad and we're working on making sure she's completely tired for a reasonable time (it may not work for Ruby but BOY does it work for Adam and I, we're zonked by the time we get to bed).

Monday, 17th July

Aggie - Ruby is excited about having a day out! She's eaten well and I've sun-blocked her and sent the bottle in case of swimming or spills. I've also included a couple of changes because she insisted on her long-sleeved top and I think it's too warm for this weather but she was determined to wear it! Hope it's a good day.

Hannah here, lovely day we had a drive to Pepperham House, went round the gardens, had a picnic in the grounds (the children loved watching the ducks) and then drove to the Palisade for another walk and icecream. They've behaved beautifully and Ruby very bravely ignored a small dog that ran up to her barking. She stuck her fingers in her ears and shouted, "BAD DOG!" It startled both owner and dog and they hurried away which we were grateful for as it shouldn't have been running around without a lead!

All of Ruby's work is coming home with her she's got rather a lot so I'm afraid

you have 2 carrier bags rather than 1 like most of the others.

Such a tired but happy girl; Ruby was all smiles but her eyes were quite 'pink' and she yawned her way through tea. In bed and fast asleep by 8.30 and we only had to change her twice each time she was asleep as soon as we tucked her in. Must be the sea air.

Tuesday, 18th July

Last day's here and Ruby's in a lovely, mellow mood after her good sleep. She's eaten well and I've sun-blocked her in case they're playing out today.

Please find cards and presents for yourself and all the staff and helpers Adam and I are so grateful for all the care and attention you've given Ruby. It's brought her on in leaps and bounds and we very much hope she'll be as happy in her next class as she has been in this one. We look forward to seeing you at the Summer Fayre on Saturday.

Once again, thank you, for everything.

Aggie & Adam

Hannah here, thank both of you so much for your lovely present and chocolates, the helpers send their thanks for your gifts to them. Although we're sad to lose Ruby it's wonderful to see her progressing so well. We all hope to see her do even more in her new class and wish her all the best for the future. There's a note here from Marion.

Very best wishes,
                    Hannah

****

Dear Parents and Children,

It was wonderful to meet you all during this last week in the infant class and I very much look forward to working with you all in the coming year. Term commences on Monday, 4th September and I and my team will be working hard in the coming weeks to make sure our new class is ready and waiting for our first day.
Have a wonderful summer,
                    Marion

****

extract from Annual Report for Ruby Redd June 1995

SOCIAL SKILLS

Dressing/undressing - Ruby can undress herself without any help, although she does not always do this at the appropriate time nor in the appropriate place! She tries hard to dress herself but still needs help to find the neck of a jumper, and to put her socks and shoes on.

Drinking - Ruby can pour a drink and knows when to stop. She can give the drinks to her friends without spilling any. She can ask for a drink without a symbol prompt 'drink'

Toilet/grooming - Ruby is almost independent in this area. She sometimes needs a prompt to stay in the toilet area until she is fully dressed again. Ruby still needs help to wash and dry her hands.

Eating - Ruby eats her dinner with a spoon and fork. She sits quietly and waits patiently for her dinner to arrive, having made some choices about the food she would like.

Independence/road sense - Ruby walks along the road in a sensible manner holding another child's hand. When allowed to walk by herself in safe areas, she stays with the main group, never running off.

GENERAL COMMENTS

Ruby is generally happy and content in the Infants. She has found a number of favourite toys to play with and can keep herself occupied in her free choice times, e.g. bathing/dressing dolly. She still needs to carry a small toy around with her but this she readily gives to an adult at work times or on request, rarely making a fuss.

Ruby has made great strides this year in all areas, particularly in her use of appropriate speech and comprehension. We are all delighted with her progress and will be sorry to lose her to another class. We wish her well and know she will continue to build on these achievements....

****

In popular tradition a story which begins 'once upon a time' ends 'and they all lived happily every after'. This is not that sort of story.

Within these pages I have tried to give an insight on what two years in the life of our 'Ruby' was like in her early childhood, using old message books as inspiration for a fictional narrative. The support and assistance described are real, so are the sometimes challenging events and so, sadly, are the examples of failure to offer help. Only any sense of order is unreal; like most lives our family's day-to-day experiences are chaotic and subject to the whims of fate and limitations of our own behaviour and needs.

An incredibly insensitive man once told me that if he had a child like Ruby he would have himself sterilised. From the way he spoke I presumed he intended to suggest her severe learning disability/autistic spectrum needs made her somehow 'damaged goods' and not worth offering a chance of life and I snapped an off-the-cuff response.

Others have suggested (more kindly) that we have 'done enough' or 'more than can be expected' and that it is time to 'think about ourselves', in other words accept that things will never change for Ruby and place her in the care of statutory services.

Our "Ruby" and other young people like her contain the same possibilities and capacity for growth and development as anybody else. Many of the barriers to achieving those personal milestones are the barriers that we, as a society, impose upon them with our expectations and judgements. I wrote this story to highlight what it is possible to achieve where appropriate help is offered and real attention is paid to what individuals with disabilities express (or show) that they want for themselves.

Public figures generally often refer to the 'costs of disability' as if the provision of care is a zero-sum game where meeting the needs of disabled citizens takes away something from others in society. It reminds me of the scenario of a favourite Grimm's fairytale of my childhood, "The old man and his grandson." To those unfamiliar with the story an old man who lives with his son, daughter-in-law and grandson has become so frail that he spills the soup he is given and is exiled from the table and served his food in a trough. The old man's son observes the grandson playing with pieces of wood and asks what he is doing.

"I'm making a trough for you and my mother to eat out of when I have grown big, you are old and I have to look after you", the grandson replies.

At the next meal the old man is restored to the table and is served from dishes together with the rest of his family.

I would argue that provision of properly funded public services which support and enable individuals to develop their full potential and protect their dignity offers an opportunity to create jobs for support workers, fosters potential new economic activity for individuals otherwise marginalised from participation in society, acts as a role model of social responsibility and good citizenship for children and young people while also carrying out the letter (and spirit) of existing legislation. As you can probably tell it is a subject close to my heart.

I hope that you have enjoyed reading 'Ruby Redd' and wish you well.

Proof

Made in the USA
Charleston, SC
01 July 2012